Plexus, London

THREE GUITARS
FOUR BOYS
5 SECONDS OF SUMMER

Contents

Introduction

Not. A. Boy. Band.

'There's something serious going on, because the fans are rabid . . . and there's a lot of them.'

the Guardian

In December 2012, the *Sydney Morning Herald* ran a feature dedicated to 'the new wave of Australian boybands,' all of them 'plotting to replicate the success of One Direction'. Amongst these home-grown acts, however – ranging from the sweet and suave What About Tonight to the ripped rude boys of the Janoskians – were four fresh faces that didn't quite fit.

Almost halfway down the page – amidst a sea of salon-perfect side-swept hair and matching ox-blood suits – came the first mention of 'high-school breakthrough' band 5 Seconds of Summer. Clad in plaid and vintage skating hoodies, and grinning ever-so-slightly awkwardly for the camera, Luke, Michael, Cal and Ash stood out from the crowd in more ways than one. Aside from their handsome guy-you-*wished*-lived-next-door good looks, 5 Seconds of Summer (or 5SOS as they've come to be known by their ever-growing army of adoring fans) have never aspired to be anyone other than themselves. Even back then, it was an approach that was working for them.

By the time the *Herald* feature went live, 5SOS had already secured the services of a stellar management team, netted a publishing deal with Sony, headlined two super-charged mini-tours of their native Oz, supported Hot Chelle Rae on the Australian leg of their world tour and scored a top-three hit with their debut EP. Yet, the article made no mention of any of this because, as far as the *Herald* was concerned, these achievements were overshadowed by a single fact. '5SOS received a priceless international boost when One Direction tweeted their video, "Gotta Get Out,"' reported the paper. Of course, this incredible stroke of luck within the Twittersphere – a veritable golden ticket to success – was already bringing 5SOS exposure

Rocking the red carpet at the Billboard Music Awards in Las Vegas, 18 May 2014.

Above: Acting out: 5SOS visit Pennsylvania's Q102 Performance Theater, August 2014. Right: Guitar heroes: 5SOS play the 2014 Billboard Music Awards, held at the MGM Grand Arena in Vegas.

beyond their wildest dreams. Yet, what the paper didn't report – and couldn't possibly have known – was that 5SOS's feelings on the subject were somewhat complicated . . .

In fact, One Direction's interest in 5SOS went way beyond a tweet. At the time of printing, the band's respective management teams were already embroiled in transpacific negotiations as to the possibility of 5 Seconds of Summer opening for One Direction on the UK, North American, and Australasian legs of their Take Me Home world tour. What would have shocked the *Herald* still further was 5SOS's ambivalent reaction to the arrangement. Torn between the magnitude of the opportunity and the need to stay true to their guitar-obsessed pop-punk roots, certain members of 5SOS were not at all convinced that they wanted to be appearing on the same stage as a boyband – even such an accomplished one as 1D. Fortunately for their fans, the chance to play in front of 15,000-strong crowds in stadiums and arenas around the globe was simply too good an opportunity to pass up. Putting their reservations to one side, 5SOS prepared to hit the road in pursuit of their dreams.

Of course, there's been a certain degree of backlash, because ever since they were officially announced as 1D's support act of choice on Valentine's Day 2013, the boys have had to defend themselves against being labelled both 'a boyband' and the 'new One Direction'.

Luke, Michael, Calum and Ash's heroes while growing up in the Western Sydney suburbs and honing their musical skills were, of course, anything but conventional boybands. Favouring Nirvana over 'N Sync, the rocky riffs of Green Day, Blink-182 and All Time Low are what

Not. A. Boy. Band.

got them through the hardest times at Norwest High School. Even so, 5SOS are no more comfortable with comparisons with Green Day et al. They don't want to be known as the 'new' anyone – good-time guys Luke, Michael, Cal and Ash are simply striving to be accepted for who they are today . . . whilst bringing a little sunshine into the lives of their fans, of course.

The fans – or the '5SOSFam' as they're collectively known – become even more defensive at the mention of the 'b word', as the *Guardian*'s Harriet Gibsone discovered while speaking to a gaggle of female 5SOSers loitering in doorways close to BBC Broadcasting House in early July 2014. 'Not. A. Boy. Band!!' chorused the girls – all gathered in the hope of catching a glimpse of their idols as they emerged from their radio interview.

In view of UK station Radio One's claim that rock music is long overdue a return to the airwaves, coupled with the 'waning popularity of *X Factor*-generated boybands', Gibsone mooted the idea that 5SOS could just turn out to be the 'blueprint for the next generation of music industry success stories'. And here's hoping that she's correct.

The signs are promising, because while the phenomenal success One Direction have enjoyed resulted in a tsunami-surge in *X Factor* franchise applications, 5 Seconds of Summer's even more rapid rise from YouTube crooners to a chart-topping act has undoubtedly seen an influx in sales of guitars and drums around the world. After all, how many bands can boast going 'straight from playing empty cinemas to sold-out stadiums . . .?'

Mick O'Shea

Chapter One

Daring to Dream

'We're a four-piece band from Western Sydney with myself, our lead vocalist and guitar player; Calum Hood, on bass and vocals; Michael Clifford on guitar and vocals; and Ashton Irwin playing drums and percussion with some vocals. We're all still trying to juggle this with school, but we're making it work as best we can.'

Luke

Dreamy blond frontman Luke Hemmings describes his band – the spectacular 5 Seconds of Summer – as a 'four-piece from Western Sydney'. Of course, he's correct, but 'Western Sydney' covers a vast amount of Australian terrain, cities and towns. In fact, Luke and his bandmates do not all hail from exactly the same place. Luke comes from Freeman's Reach, Michael lived in Quaker's Hill, Calum grew up between the two in Riverstone and Ashton spent most of his childhood in Windsor.

Luke, Michael and Calum all attended Norwest Christian College in Riverstone, an exclusive local school that charges thousands of dollars worth of fees every year. For the sum of $16,000 to $20,000 per pupil, the school's teaching staff aim to work 'respectfully, thoughtfully and prayerfully' to support their students on their journey to becoming remarkable young people.

This was certainly true of music teacher Adam Day, who acted as a mentor to three guitar-obsessed Year Sevens. To the irritation of his colleagues, the future 5SOSers appeared far more interested in learning chord structures and choruses than their ABCs. Even so, Day went the extra mile to encourage them in following their dreams, perhaps because – rather than chasing fifteen fickle minutes of fame as contestants on *The X Factor* or *Australian Idol* – the hard-working trio remained dedicated to honing their skills on guitar.

Left: Backstage at Stockholm's Friends Arena, Sweden, 14 June 2014. Below: 5SOS plus Q102: Luke, Mikey, Ash and Cal visit Pennsylvania's legendary performance theater, April 2014.

Italian SOS: Mikey, Ash, Cal and Luke greet their public from an elegant Milanese balcony, June 2014.

Not so far away, their future bandmate Ashton was putting in hours of practise to perfect his drumming technique. Unlike the Norwest boys, Ash actually did attempt the X *Factor* fast-track to fame, applying to appear in the Australian version of the talent show in 2010. Although he failed to make an impression, the rejection would ultimately prove a blessing in disguise. Altiyan Childs, who went on to win the competition, enjoyed two huge Australian hits in the afterglow – a single entitled 'Somewhere in the World' and an eponymous debut album – before disappearing from the scene altogether. Rumour has it that he retreated from the spotlight in order to 'reconnect with his sadness'.

Unlike Ash – who's always been a cheeky presence onstage – Luke, Michael and Calum were a little less confident about showcasing their talents. 'I started teaching them in Year Seven,' Day told the *Sydney Morning Herald* in April 2014 in the wake of 5 Seconds of Summer's *She Looks So Perfect* EP debuting at number two on the *Billboard 200*. 'They excelled in all the practical activities of music, but were very quiet, shy, and reserved. They were very much closet musos.

'I wrote on their reports back then that it would be good to seek performance opportunities to develop their confidence,' he added. 'They've certainly done that – more than any other student I've ever said that to!'

Under Day's tutelage, Luke, Michael and Calum soon began to stand out from the crowd at Norwest. Although they occasionally needed to be pushed to perform in front of their peers, the boys have never been afraid to dream big. Michael has always been not-so-quietly confident about his future in the music industry. Indeed, Adam Day remembers how, '[He] always said to me, "I'm going to be a superstar one day". He said that from Year Nine on. I remember him coming off stage from a performance one evening and he said, "Yeah, that's what I'm going to do. I'm going to be famous one day."

'They're highly accomplished in what they're doing, mostly in guitar,' he continued. 'They don't just dance in front of a backing track. They're really skilled on their instruments.'

Yet even Day – who now teaches music at a private Christian college in the coastal town of Taree, New South Wales – is staggered by just how far his three ex-pupils have come in so short a space of time. 'I can't drive to school without hearing them on the radio now,' he said. 'It's quite bizarre to hear your students on the radio. I can see the road they're on, and I think they'll go right to the top. I wouldn't be surprised if they're able to make it in America as well.'

As the boys' former teacher, Day is proud of the incredible chart progress 5SOS have made to date. As for the question of whether 5SOS are the sort to let fame go to their heads? Day

> 'Luke was posting videos on YouTube and stuff . . .
> and it was like, "Dude, let's make a band."'
>
> Mike

stressed that, 'At [Norwest] we tried to teach them a lot of values,' he added. 'And I really hope they can remember them and are able to keep a good life balance.'

While Luke, Michael and Calum were all showing great promise, Luke's reluctance to blow his own trumpet in the classroom meant that no one at Norwest – least of all Adam Day – was aware that he'd taken to videoing himself covering songs from the radio and posting these videos on YouTube under his 'hemmo1996' personal account.

Speaking with the *New York Times* in July 2014, Luke revealed that his passion for music started even before he got to Norwest.

'What really got me into music is the band Good Charlotte when I was ten,' he revealed. 'And then it grew into Green Day with *American Idiot*. I had the Foo Fighters' *Live at Hyde Park* DVD and my dad had the AC/DC box set.

'I used to watch them all the time. I had the Slash *How to Play Guitar* DVD. I just wanted to be the best guitarist, like, ever. My brother played guitar and he taught me "Smoke on the Water," and I played it over and over again for ages.'

Green Day would also feature heavily in Calum's musical education. 'When I was about fourteen, I got on the bus, and my sister's friend's brother handed me a burnt CD that said "American Idiot,"' he explained to the same newspaper. 'That was pretty much the first time that I fell in love with music. I couldn't stop listening to it. I saw an acoustic guitar sitting around the house and I picked it up.'

★★★★

Now that 5 Seconds of Summer are a hot new band and Luke is one of the most recognisable teenagers on the planet, his posting videos on YouTube seems perfectly standard, but back when he was just hemmo1996 – a schoolboy from Norwest – it was a very brave move indeed. Even the least talented *X Factor* wannabe must admit to having warbled in the shower, behind closed doors; yet here was Luke exposing himself to potential ridicule.

Luke's first YouTube offering came on 3 February 2011, when he posted his version of Michael Posner's recent hit 'Please Don't Go'. Later that same month he posted two videos in the same day: one was a cover of Mayday Parade's 'Jersey' (complete with guitar accompaniment) and the second was a cover of Bruno Mars' 'Just the Way You Are'. These were followed up the following month with covers of Cee Lo Green's 'Forget You' and Ron Pope's 'Fireflies'.

Luke's postings quickly became the talk of the school and it wasn't long before the news reached certain enthusiastic ears. According to 5SOS folklore, 11 April 2011 is the day Calum and Michael first approached Luke with the idea of their doing something together.

> 'Michael didn't like Luke at first and I was best friends with Michael at the time, so I actually didn't like him.'
>
> Calum

'Luke was posting videos on YouTube and stuff,' Michael subsequently told *Vevo* magazine. 'And it was like, "Dude, let's make a band."'

In interviews, Luke has previously become all warm and fuzzy about his bandmates, describing 5SOS as a 'proper little family' and anyone looking at photos of the boys together would assume they've always been as close as any blood-related brothers could be. This wasn't always the case, however, as Calum revealed in one of the videos posted by the band online. His shocking revelation was that, 'Michael didn't like Luke at first and I was best friends with Michael at the time, so I actually didn't like him,' he explained. 'But in the back of my mind I was like, "He seems a really cool guy."'

'It's true,' Michael himself affirmed. 'In Year Nine [Luke and I] hated each other. He wanted to kill me and I wanted to kill him. Somehow, in Year Ten we became best friends.'

Four days on, Luke introduced his new collaborators to his fans on YouTube. Then came several weeks of secret jamming sessions . . . after which the boys decided they were ready to go public. In early June, they posted an acoustic version of Blink-182's 2004 hit, 'I Miss You'.

Needless to say, initial support and encouragement came from family and friends, all of whom enthusiastically spread the word about the YouTube video wherever and whenever they could.

Buoyed by this ever-growing network of support, Luke, Michael, and Calum sat down to work out the chord structure to 'If It Means a Lot to You' by A Day to Remember (from the metalcore act's 2009 album, *Homesick*).

Calum was away on a family holiday so didn't appear in the video for this track when it was posted some three weeks later on 1 July, but he was back in the frame for an acoustic version of Chris Brown's 2011 hit 'Next To You' (originally featuring Justin Bieber). This, of course, is the video which set the boys on the path to superstardom, racking up an unbelievable 600,000 hits by the end of the year. It has since gone on to rack up in excess of 1.5 million . . .

Life in different colours: Luke, Mikey, Ash and Cal (clockwise from top-left)
rock stadiums everywhere from London to Michigan to Milan, 2013-14.

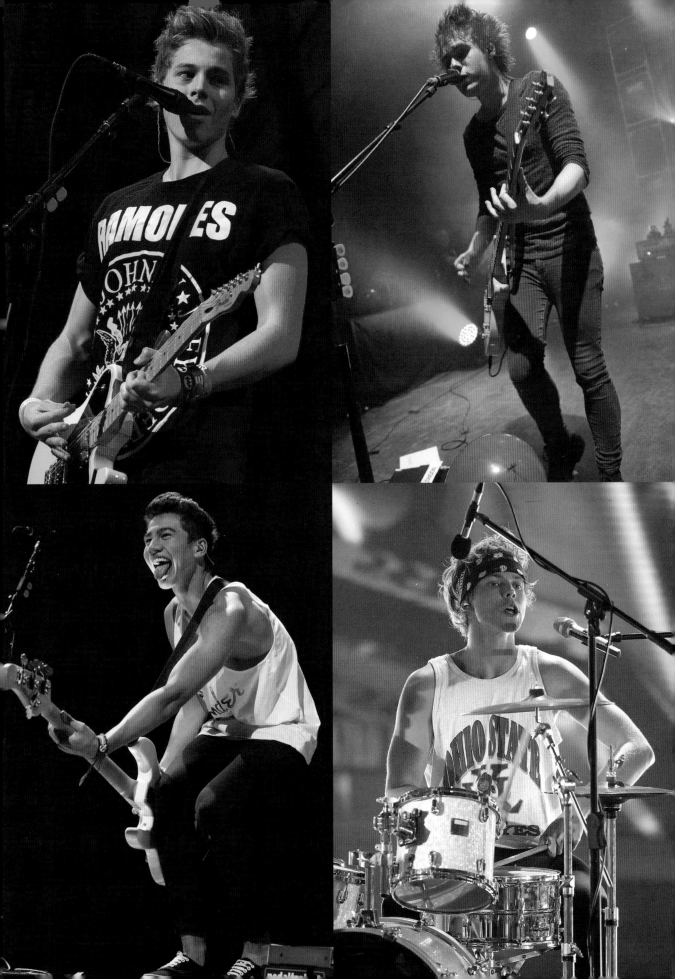

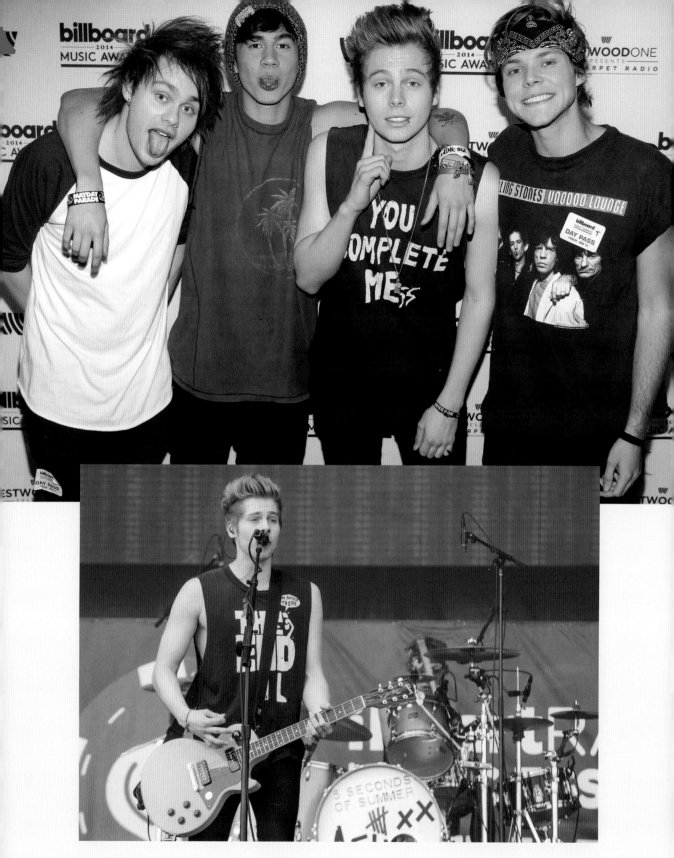

Say what? 5SOS hit the red carpet at the 2014 Billboard Music Awards (above) whilst Luke steals the spotlight at the iHeartRadio Festival (below), September 2014.

'Next To You' would prove Michael's last pre-5SOS contribution to YouTube, as the next posting, on 28 July, featured Luke and Calum covering Go Radio's 'Forever My Father' from the Florida-based outfit's 2011 album, *Lucky Street*.

'[A] new cover that we quickly did at school for you guys,' they posted on their YouTube account. 'Thanks for all your support guys, love you all! Another cover should be hittin you guys up soon ♥'

Three days later the guys proved as good as their word by posting a video of Luke giving a solo performance of Ron Pope's 2009 single, 'A Drop in the Ocean'. Once again, Calum

`'Riverstone is proper violent, which made us stick together.`
`And that's what grew our bond together, because when we met,`
`we realised we're the same. We don't necessarily belong.'`

Ash

provided accompaniment on a version of British singer Adele's massive *Billboard* number one, 'Rolling in the Deep', which was, of course, covered and released as a single later that same year (2011) by Linkin Park.

The performances were as crude as the video editing and at times the boys forgot the lyrics or hit the wrong note. None of this mattered to those tuning into YouTube to view the latest offering, however. As far as they were concerned, the bum notes and bloopers merely added to the boys' charm.

★★★★

Growing up in and around the neat yet nondescript Sydney commuter suburb of Riverstone has undoubtedly given Luke, Michael and Calum the 'good life balance' to which Adam Day was referring. Originally settled at the turn of the nineteenth century as part of a government stock farm, Riverstone is one of the oldest towns in Australia. Despite sizeable tracts of land being given over to cope with a housing boom at the start of the twenty-first century, at the 2011 census Riverstone had an estimated population of just 6,191 souls.

Nevertheless, Riverstone has its fair share of troublemakers – and they certainly made life difficult for 5SOS. Speaking with the *Guardian* in July 2014, Ashton – though not strictly from Riverstone (Ashton hails from Windsor) – told how he has been 'nearly' stabbed on more than one occasion. '[Riverstone is] proper violent, which made us stick together,' he revealed. 'And that's what grew our bond together, because when we met, we realised we're the same. We don't necessarily belong.'

'"She Looks So Perfect" was about running away a little bit,' Luke said in the same interview. 'It wasn't our favourite place, where we grew up. We're never going to write an "American Idiot" song; we're not going to write about politics – maybe when we're older,' he went on. 'We write about being a social outcast, as well as girls and stuff.'

Whatever 5SOS felt about their hometown, however, they have the close-knit Riverstone community – in which gossip can't fail to travel – to thank for the significant break waiting just around the corner.

Luke Hemmings Fact File

Birth Date: 16 July 1996

Star sign: Cancer

Secret SOS: 'I carry a hairbrush with me.'

Words to live by: 'Find something that makes you happy and don't let anyone take it away from you.'

Luke Robert Hemmings was born 16 July 1996, under the sign of Cancer the crab. People born on this day are generally very intuitive and wise, with all the emotional sensitivity that being a Cancerian brings. With the ruling astrological planet for this particular day being Neptune, Luke was blessed with a brilliant imagination that's perfect for penning dreamy lyrics. Another Cancerian talent of his is being able to accurately size-up both people and his surroundings in an instant.

As anyone who's watched a 5SOS interview will know, shy-guy Luke can be very self-sacrificing, yet extremely sociable and warm with passionate ideals and views about music, the world – everything. Michael, Calum and Ashton would all agree with this assessment, as they have described their leader as 'shy', 'serious', and 'sensible'.

Cancerians can be prone to occasional displays of uncharacteristically crazy behaviour whenever you least expect it and Luke is no exception. Whether he's stripping off in front of their tour-bus driver in America or giving interviews in his underwear, Luke's quirky (not to mention swoon-inducing) tendency to act out is just part of the reason that we love him so.

Luke was born and raised in Freeman's Reach, Western Sydney. He is still extremely close to both his parents, Andrew and Liz, and enjoys a special bond with his two older brothers,

Rise and shine: Luke gets up close and personal on UK TV show, This Morning, June 2014.

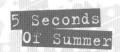

Ben and Jack. Although 5SOS's hectic touring schedule has tested the Hemmings family ties, Luke returns to Freeman's Reach whenever he can. Out of all the 5SOS boys, Luke was the only one to return home for an Aussie Christmas following the band's song-writing trip to London in December 2012.

The Hemmings are a typical Australian family in that they all take an active interest in sports – particularly winter sports. Luke himself is a talented snowboarder with some serious moves on the piste.

Liz Hemmings was once a maths teacher and while Luke showed an early aptitude for the subject, it soon became apparent to all who knew him that music was his one and only passion – especially after one of his brothers taught him the tell-tale opening riff to Deep Purple's 'Smoke on the Water'.

When Liz and Andrew first got married, Guns N' Roses and grunge still ruled the airwaves . . . perhaps this is the reason they bought Luke the *Slash: How to Play Guitar* DVD. The first

> 'My least favourite thing about being in a band is being away.
> It's actually a good thing as well because you get to travel, but it's
> also sad because you don't get to see your family as much.'
>
> Luke

album Luke bought with his own pocket money was Good Charlotte's 2002 release, *The Young and the Hopeless*. To this day, the American pop-punk five-piece remain one of his favourite bands. By his own admission, however, it was Green Day's multi-platinum, multi-award-winning album *American Idiot* (released September 2004) that truly gripped his imagination.

Luke's all-time hero is Green Day's manic-eyed frontman, Billie Joe Armstrong. Despite 5SOS having visited Los Angeles on several occasions of late, their paths have yet to cross. Luke believes this is a good thing as he'd 'probably cry'.

Blubbering in front of his idols could become a something of a habit for Luke. During an interview with the New Zealand-based *Coup de Main* magazine in April 2013, he was asked to choose between being related to Kurt Cobain or Dave Grohl. Faced with this 'tough choice', Luke eventually opted for Grohl as they'd be able to talk about Nirvana *and* the Foo Fighters. Should this amazing opportunity ever arise, however, Luke admitted that he'd 'definitely cry' (not just probably).

This same interview found Luke in a playful mood, as he also confided that his 'friendship crush' would be Will Smith, and that his spirit animal would be a whale so that he could 'be a big fish in a little pond'.

Hearing their offspring declare they were going to be the new Billie Joe Armstrong would have most parents reaching for the smelling salts, but Liz and Andrew both recognised their son had found his calling and enrolled him at the fee-paying Norwest Christian College where his creativity could be channelled. For, while Norwest is not a 'fame' school per se, the faculty openly encourages its musically-minded pupils in organising impromptu concerts

Luke poses with members of the 5SOSFam outside of the MGM Grand Arena, Las Vegas, April 2014.

and setting up guitars and amplifiers in the grounds.

Aside from meeting his best friends and soon-to-be 5SOS bandmates Michael and Calum at Norwest, Luke would also meet Aleisha McDonald, the first girl who – as Luke himself told *Top of the Pops* magazine – 'liked him and was comfortable in her own skin'.

Like Luke, Aleisha was a budding singer-songwriter, and although the two initially just hung out together talking about music, their relationship quickly blossomed into romance. From that point on they were virtually inseparable. Indeed, the cute couple would often

'Our influences are more rock acts and it's special that we've got that bond from school. Being put together wouldn't have worked for us.'

Luke

Luke Hemmings

perform together – at school, for family and friends and more. They even uploaded several videos to YouTube; the standouts being Maroon 5's 'She Will Be Loved' and 'If It Means A Lot to You' by A Day to Remember, which Luke would also cover with Michael.

Aleisha definitely meant a lot to Luke and their relationship carried on beyond their final year at Norwest. But with his commitments to 5 Seconds of Summer taking up more and more of his time, the two decided it best to call it a day. They remain good friends, however, and Luke's feelings for Aleisha have never truly diminished. When he was asked via a Twitter Q&A to name the best thing that had ever happened to him outside the band, he didn't hesitate for a moment. 'Probably my ex-girlfriend,' he answered.

As Luke's profile rose, so – somewhat inevitably – did Aleisha's. 'Luke is absolutely the most perfect and amazing person I've ever met,' she told Ask.fm. 'He is such a nice boy and a good friend – still my best friend.'

Due to his ongoing 5SOS commitments, Luke's studies were also beginning to suffer (with the exception of music, of course, in which Luke was always an 'A' student). Prior to his hooking up with Michael and Calum, he'd been predicted excellent grades across the board. Despite Liz's best efforts (she did all she could to provide support at home and on the road), something simply had to give ... and as far as Luke was concerned, it wasn't going to be 5SOS.

In hindsight, Liz and Andrew's concerns about Luke jeopardising his future seem a total overreaction, but at the time they were very real. True, the boys were already playing sold-out shows in their native Sydney and other major cities across Australia, but there was no real interest in 5SOS outside of Australasia, and the leg-up they were to receive from One Direction's Louis Tomlinson was still several months away.

When the world finally did sit up and take notice of 5 Seconds of Summer following the soar-away success of 'She Looks So Perfect', it was, as is customary, the band's frontman who was singled out for special attention.

Having labelled him 'the Heartthrob', *Billboard* magazine waxed lyrical about Luke's 'perfectly-coiffed blond hair', his 'disarming smile' and 'devastating blue eyes', while his HSP (Harry Styles Potential) was deemed 'off the charts'.

Michael might be the one who enjoys all the attention over his ever-changing hair colour, but he says that it's Luke who actually spends the most time in front of the mirror.

'He's 75 inches tall; without [the quiff] he's 71 inches,' he playfully told reporters. 'It's a four-inch quiff!'

Somewhat surprisingly, the *Billboard* article neglected to mention Luke's slender, six-foot frame in its gushy tribute to 5SOS, but this is not something to be taken for granted. To look at him now it's hard to believe, but Luke claims to have been a 'bit chubby' as a child. Even now, he still loves his food and comes in for a fair amount of ribbing for his huge appetite. According to his bandmates, Luke is the one who can put away two dinners, wash a large tub of popcorn down with a jumbo drink at the cinema and maybe even stop off for a snack on the way home.

As if to prove his hungry-boy prowess, Luke scooped first prize in the 5SOS Pizza Hut ice-cream eating challenge, after devouring an incredible seventeen bowls!

With teeth: onstage at London's Shepherd's Bush Empire, March 2014.

Chapter Two

They Look So Perfect

'Michael sent a Facebook message to Ashton who he knew
through one of our friends and was like, "Hey man,
there's gonna be so many people at the gig we just
booked. How would you like to come drum with us?" And
Ashton was like, "Hell yeah, that sounds sick!"'

Luke

Regrettably, Luke, Michael and Calum's combined efforts on YouTube were winning them no kind of kudos in the classroom.

'I think we sort of gravitated towards each other 'cause we were like the outcasts at school,' Ash told *Vevo* magazine in July 2014. 'It just wasn't cool what we were doing. No one thought that it was special or anything like that and no one really cared.'

Fortunately, the boys remained undaunted. Rather than post another video, however, they decided it was time to take things to the next level. Via Facebook, they announced they'd be appearing in 'An Afternoon at the Cinema – Unplugged' on Saturday, 17 September, as support for the popular Adelaide four-piece, Some Time Soon. Thanks to Michael, the talented threesome already had a name that could be featured in the promo material . . .

Soon after joining forces on YouTube, Calum, Luke and Michael had realised they were in need of a name. Rather than spend hours obsessing over what they should be called, the idea of 5 Seconds of Summer came randomly into Michael's head. Struck with inspiration, he reached for his mobile – and the rest is 5SOS history. 'I sent Luke and Calum a message and said, "Hey boys, I'm naming the band 5 Seconds of Summer," and they were like, "Okay, we're cool with that."'

Calum subsequently expanded on this during an interview with the Australian news show, *60 Minutes* in July 2014: 'I remember we were in science class when we were probably fifteen and just writing a bunch of band names on a piece of paper . . . not paying any attention to anything the teacher was saying.

Left and below: at the end of their super-charged gig at New York's iHeartRadio Theater, Ash hands his sticks to a girl in the crowd, July 2014.

'We hated every one of them. Michael went away and texted us. He was like, "how about the name 5 Seconds of Summer?" We were all like, "yeah alright. That's fine." When you're in a band in school, you never think it's going to amount to much . . . you just pick your name.'

Luke also let slip one of the names being bandied around during science class. 'There was a non-serious one that was kind of a joke,' he revealed. 'It was called "Bromance".'

5 Seconds of Summer were quite literally the newest kids on the block, yet Some Time Soon were not. In the five years they'd been together, they'd already toured Australia extensively and released their first EP. Even so, the promoters chose to advertise the free show as 'two Australian up-and-comers'.

> 'Michael texted us, he was like, "how about the name 5 Seconds of Summer?" We were all like, "alright, that's fine". When you're in a band in school, you just pick your name because you're not expecting it to last very long.'
>
> Calum

Rather than stress over the writing of new material at short notice, the boys focused their energies on perfecting their repertoire of YouTube covers. They were understandably nervous in the days leading up to their first ever gig. But on the night itself, Luke, Michael, and Calum took to the stage like seasoned pros, and received a thoroughly deserved enthusiastic ovation.

After the show, they took to Facebook to thank everyone who had come along specifically to see them and to ask those who'd taken photos or videos to 'be sure to tag our page in it'.

★★★★

Luke, Michael and Calum were still buzzing from their cinema show when they received an invitation to play one of Sydney's coolest rock venues, the Annandale Hotel. Evidently impressed by what he'd seen and heard of them on YouTube, the Annandale's manager messaged the boys on Facebook, offering them a slot on Saturday, 3 December.

They could have played the Annandale as a three-piece, but instead Luke, Michael and Calum saw it as a crucial chance to complete their band. This, of course, meant finding a drummer.

Faced with slim pickings at Norwest, the boys recognised they'd need to cast their net a little further in the search for their ideal sticksman. 'We had a gig booked and after we got the gig we were like, "We haven't even got a drummer",' Michael told *Vevo* in July 2014. 'I knew Ashton; he went to a school near us and I was like, "Hey man, do you wanna play a gig to two hundred people?" And he was like, "Yeah, I do!"'

They had their drummer, but Ash's inclusion meant they'd also need someone to play bass – as a complement to Ash's percussion. Rather than recruit an outsider, Calum – who'd always considered himself less talented than either Luke or Michael on guitar – volunteered for the role. This would require the purchase of a new four-string bass. But while he saved up enough money for the purpose, Calum was smart enough to improvise by playing the bottom E string on his acoustic six-string instrument.

At eighteen, Ash was two years older than his new-found bandmates. He also had something of a reputation on the local music scene. Aside from having drummed in several bands, he'd also been one half of an acoustic duo named Swallow the Goldfish.

Even before they hooked up for 5SOS, Luke was vaguely acquainted with Ash, since Ash once rescued shy-guy Luke from a majorly awkward social situation. Behind the scenes at 5SOS's *Cioè* photo-shoot in June 2014, Luke gave his version of events. 'It's not that dramatic,' he shrugged. 'I was with some people that I didn't really like too much and Ashton was along with them, but I didn't know him then 'cause I didn't know if I liked him or not.

'The people that I was with, I'd just got a haircut and they were teasing me about it. Ashton was like, "leave the boy alone".'

Luke, Michael and Calum were already rehearsing four evenings a week, but even as the new guy, Ash sensed that this might not be enough to help them stand out from the hundreds of other wannabes. The older, more experienced drummer insisted they up the ante by rehearsing six evenings a week. Unlike his new bandmates, he'd been a face on Sydney's thriving live music scene long enough to realise that they were up against some tough competition. 'Sydney underground bands and [Sydney] bands in general are very heavy,' he later told *Rock Sound*. 'It's very hardcore, and we wanted to be a rock band like Green Day.

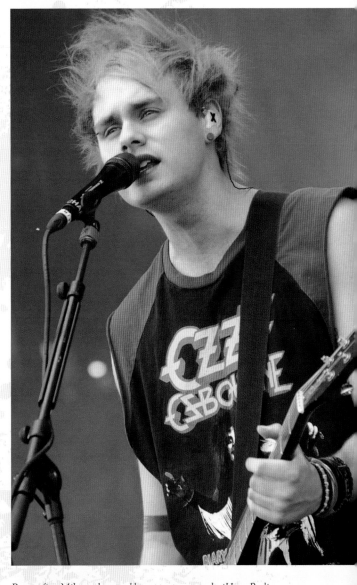

Boy on fire: Mike makes a red-hot appearance at the iHeartRadio Music Festival, Las Vegas, September 2014.

'We didn't really fit,' he added. 'The different thing with us was that girls would come to see us. [The other bands'] crowds would just be sweaty dudes and they hated us.'

They'd started penning their own material the moment Ash joined and, in order to tighten up their act even further, the boys set about practising their new tracks in the dark – no mean feat, as any musician will tell you. 'I know it sounds weird but it worked,' Michael later revealed. 'We thought if we can't see what we are doing and we can still play then we might sound good when the lights are turned on.'

Once again, 5 Seconds of Summer had the pleasure of seeing their name splashed across a publicity poster. And as the day of the Annandale show approached they posted several messages on their Facebook page. On 29 November they wrote:

Hey guys, our gig is comin up this saturday at annandale hotel in sydney (: hope you guys can make it, we'll be performing some of our originals, plus some covers. You can buy tickets cheaper than at the door from the link below . . . peace out homedawgs. X

This Annandale gig – 5SOS's very first with the four-man line-up we've grown to know and adore – was clearly a crucial one, in the minds of all the boys. How would their newly written 'originals' be received? Had they practised hard enough – with the lights on and off – to make an impression?

As Ash subsequently revealed, the reaction of the crowd that night was anything but encouraging. 'We really sucked!' he sighed. 'People hated us; they told us we were really bad every single day. We used to have to go and play shows with metal bands at the Annandale. We barely had any fans, but they were so dedicated. And coming to the Annandale when you are barely sixteen and a girl is not ideal.

'But you have to suck at the beginning,' he added philosophically. 'And you have to have crap for instruments and not be able to afford stuff and work from the bottom for the band to grow.'

Speaking with USA Today in April 2014, by which time 5SOS were seasoned pros who'd played a hundred shows or more, Ash revealed that despite the tumbleweeds drifting across the dance-floor that night, that Annandale gig is still the band's absolute favourite. 'It was a terrible gig, but there was just something about it that me and the boys loved,' he explained. 'We knew it was the start of something cool for us.'

> 'We sort of gravitated towards each other 'cause we were like the outcasts at school. It just wasn't cool what we were doing. No one thought that it was special or anything like that and no one really cared.'
>
> Luke

Next Monday, they returned to school to find they were still viewed as losers by their classmates at Norwest and Western Sydney Institute, where Ash was studying on a TAFE music course.

'5 Seconds of Summer was just a joke to them,' Ash told Vevo. 'We really worked hard to be a good band, we did everything we could to be a good credible band.

'The only attention we really got for our music skill was on YouTube,' he continued. 'The first cover we did was Wheatus' "Teenage Dirtbag". I think that song really represented what type of band we wanted to be. We didn't know it though . . . we were just sort of drawn into it.'

Inspired by an unrequited crush and sung from the perspective of the biggest loser in school, Wheatus' 2000 single may as well have been 5SOS's anthem . . .

★★★★

5 Seconds of Summer were clearly not lacking direction, but if they were ever to emulate the achievements of their heroes, then they were in serious need of professional representation; not to mention a demo tape guaranteed to get them noticed. As luck would have it, they managed to secure the former whilst checking out the latter.

During a visit to Sydney's Studios 301, the boys chatted with the studio's manager, Adam

Three reasons to love 5SOS: Ash, Cal and Mikey attend the 2014 Billboard Music Awards – but where's Luke?

Wilkinson, who unbeknownst to them had recently branched out from producing by forming his own management company, AWM Management.

Wilkinson was on the lookout for fresh Aussie talent to add to his books and 5 Seconds of Summer fitted the bill perfectly. 'I immediately liked the look of them, and wanted to work with them . . . but forgot their name,' he sheepishly revealed to *Music Network*. Thankfully for all concerned, the boys were just a couple of clicks away online. 'I took to Facebook and YouTube,' he continued, 'and finally tracked them down, eventually getting in touch with Ashton.'

Wilkinson's fears that he'd blown his chance to sign them proved unfounded, and the boys would later joke that Ashton had only responded to his Facebook entreaty because it was the first time they'd as yet been messaged by a male.

As he was new to music management, Wilkinson thought it prudent to share his duties with a more experienced partner. With the boys' backing, he approached Matt Emsell at Wonder Management, (Wilkinson had once shared an office with Emsell and been impressed with his work).

Using 'Teenage Dirtbag' as a template, the boys had built up an impressive repertoire of original pop-punk tracks, including 'Gotta Get Out' and 'Too Late'. For their first ever studio recording, however, on 21 April 2012, they opted for a cover of Blink-182's 'I Miss You'.

Wilkinson and Emsell both had A&R contacts within various record companies, but as any contract offered at this stage would heavily favour the record company, they decided that the best option would be to sign with a music publisher, allowing them to stay in full creative

control. Emsell had already had another of his acts, Amy Meredith, sign with Sony/ATV Music Publishing. Given the pop-punk style of this quirky Aussie five-piece, it seemed logical for 5SOS to follow in their footsteps . . .

It was also through Emsell's involvement with Amy Meredith that the boys were able to spend studio-time with the band's singer Christian Lo Russo and guitarist Joel Chapman. During this time, 5SOS traded ideas with the older punksters, looking at ways of expanding their own developing sound.

Thrilled to have netted a publishing deal with one of the most renowned companies in the business, the boys took to Facebook and Twitter with a vengeance. Their fans were equally stoked, but wanted to know when they might next see the band on a stage.

Now that everything was moving in a more professional direction, the boys were itching to see what Wilkinson and Emsell were planning in terms of a live tour. Again, the duo no doubt possessed the numbers for every leading booking agent in Australia on speed dial. Nonetheless, they weren't about to make use of them just yet. Fortunately for 5SOS, they were savvy enough to recognise the wisdom in holding out for the right moment.

> 'The different thing with us was that girls would come to see us. The other bands' crowds would just be sweaty dudes and they hated us.'
>
> Luke

'No one likes to hang out in an empty bar, no matter how great the music,' Emsell said at the time, possibly with the boys' December show at the Annandale Hotel foremost in his thoughts. 'The best way to experience a new band is in a small venue crammed with screaming fans – a small group of trendy tastemakers who will be the first in the world to discover this great talent. Then one day they can say, "I saw them at venue X with two hundred other people and now they're playing stadiums".'

In May, the boys announced a three-date mini tour comprising a hometown show at the Factory Theatre, as well as dates at the Old Museum in Brisbane and Xavier College in Melbourne. All three shows sold out within two minutes of going on sale. When additional shows were announced in each city to cope with the demand, these also sold out within minutes.

Within six short months, 5 Seconds of Summer had gone from playing a near-empty Annandale Hotel to selling out six 300-capacity shows in three major cities. If their heads weren't spinning already, as the opening Sydney date drew closer they received their first international press courtesy of hothits.com, who pronounced them 'the band you should be obsessing over'.

'We've only really been a band for four months, but we are hoping to begin working on our debut release of original stuff as soon as possible,' a giddy Ashton told the Aussie website musicfeeds.com that same month in the boys' first significant interview. 'We've got a bunch of writing sessions coming up and we're rehearsing a few times a week and writing all the time.

'We really just want to get it right for our fans and give them something they want,' he added. 'We're all pretty excited, though. Everything is coming together slowly but surely.'

Indeed it was . . .

He looks so perfect: Luke, breaking hearts at the 2014 Billboard Music Awards.

Michael Clifford
Fact File

Birth Date: 20 November 1995
Star sign: Scorpio
Secret SOS: 'I'm very OCD about things.
I wash my hands probably about 20 times a day.'
Words to live by: 'If you can't be naked, what can you be?'

Michael Gordon Clifford, or 'Mike' as he's known to his family and friends, was born on 20 November 1995, which makes him a feisty Scorpio. Scorpio boys are likely to be strong willed, determined and hungry for success. They absolutely love a challenge, but are willing to put their friends and family first, because Scorpios like caring Michael often see themselves as nurturers.

In the series of 'getting-to-know-you' videos the band posted on YouTube around the time of their Annandale Hotel gig, Luke, Cal and Ash described Mike as 'weird', 'nerdy', 'sassy', 'sloppy' and 'funny', while Cal said he was 'just a great friend overall' as he could always be relied on to cheer them up whenever they were feeling down.

A prime example of Mike's playfulness came during a Skype interview with *Coup de Main* magazine while backstage at the Leadmill in Sheffield, England, when he named his 'spirit animal' as either the 'paper-clip guy from Microsoft Word' or Pikachu from Pokémon.

His on-air confessions didn't stop there. On one occasion he's voiced his yearning to be a Pokémon in human-form because it 'would be so cool'. He also secretly wishes he could be Elizabeth from the videogame, BioShock. 'I know it sounds weird,' he chuckled, 'but I wish I was.'

*Colour me gorgeous: Mike shows off his bubblegum
locks on* This Morning, *June 2014.*

Smitten 5SOSers clamour for selfies with Michael outside BBC Radio One, London, July 2014.

'My lips are huge . . .
I'm Mangelina Jolie!'

Mike

An only child raised by a single mother (his parents Daryl and Karen are separated), Michael's never known what it is to be part of a large family – until he found fame with 5SOS. 'I actually don't like calling you guys fans because you guys are like my family I never had,' Mikey revealed in an emotional tweet in 2012. Being the only member of 5SOS not to have siblings did have some perks, however. Aside from never having to share his toys, or worry about a kid brother rummaging through his wardrobe, there was no one to argue with whenever he fancied his favourite meal (cheeseburgers), or fight for the remote while watching his all-time favourite film, *Forrest Gump*.

True to his Scorpio nature, Mike applies total dedication to everything he does in life. However, this does mean he has a tendency to overdo things and occasionally take them to the extreme – as his obsession with dyeing his hair every colour of the rainbow clearly demonstrates.

Mike is a natural blond, but since finding fame with 5SOS, his much-photographed locks have been electric blue, green, hot pink, purple and pure white, while for a time he adopted the 'reverse skunk' look: white at the sides with a black streak running down the middle. An expression of his cool, quirky personality, Mike's hair is clearly important to him as well as the 5SOSFam. Indeed, he once said that he'd rather eat an entire jar of Vegemite in one sitting than shave his head.

Another feature that Mike's particularly conscious of is his luscious pouty mouth. 'My lips are huge . . . I'm Mangelina Jolie,' he quipped on Twitter in September 2012 . . . as if the 5SOSFam hadn't noticed them already!

Like Luke and Cal, he attended Norwest Christian College. Despite Michael's admission that academia has never been his thing (during an interview with the *Daily Mail*), it will still come as a surprise to some 5SOSers to learn that the gifted guitar stringer got a 'D' in music – something which his former teacher Adam Day chose to keep to himself when speaking to the press about his former pupils.

With Luke being a fellow water sign it's surprising he and Mike didn't get on when they

'I'm just going through the colour wheel and checking out what I haven't done. Now I'm going to have to start to do patterns.'

Mike

Don't stop: Mikey works the crowd like a pro at the iHeartRadio Music Festival, Las Vegas.

first met at school. Mike also shares Luke and Calum's enthusiasm for stripping off whenever the mood takes him. 'The nakedness gets pretty bad,' he revealed in *The Hits*. '[But] if you can't be naked, what can you be? The words to live by.'

This is indeed a maxim to live by, but when he was called upon to verify the rumour that Cal wore a thong on stage, Mike tactfully chose to neither confirm nor deny the rumours. 'I think he (Cal) is a free man and he does what he pleases,' he said, before adding that he'd be 'quite scared' should the rumour turn out to be true.

'I think it would be quite breezy and feel quite nice,' he said on being quizzed as to whether he'd ever follow Cal's lead. 'It might just be a band thing now – we all play with thongs on!' Mike has since admitted to owning a set of My Little Pony underwear, but has yet to reveal whether he has worn them on stage …

Whereas Luke tends to favour Fender guitars, Mike usually plumps for the more hard-rockin' sound that only a Gibson can provide. He says this is largely due to Gibson inviting the band along to their London showroom prior to their heading up to Glasgow to kick-start their UK tour. 'We just walked into this room full of guitars – it was insane,' he said. 'They let me borrow one and I have been playing them ever since. Thank you, Gibson!'

Mike is clearly a fan of the make as his first decent guitar was an Epiphone Les Paul.

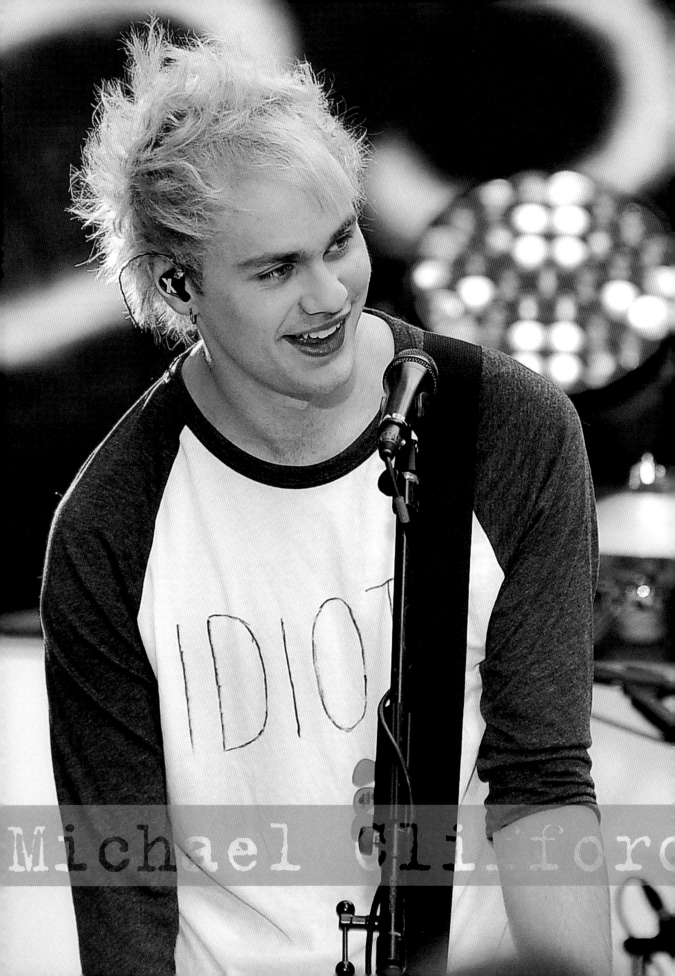

Epiphone is a subsidiary of the Gibson Guitar Corporation and, while near-identical in design to the famous Gibson Les Paul, it is more modestly priced.

His preferred Gibson axes are all signature models – a Slash Signature, a Joan Jett Signature and a Signature T Les Paul Goldtop. With the way things are going for 5SOS, it surely won't be too long before a 'Mikey Clifford Signature' goes into production.

It could also be argued that Mike has perfected a signature haircut, given that the ever-increasing number of teen guys copying his coif would have had to ask their stylist for a 'Mikey'. An edgy hairstyle has long been considered *de rigueur* in rock'n'roll – from the moment Elvis slicked back his quiff – yet while every rocker strives to do something to stand out from the crowd, few have managed it quite like Mike.

'I was just looking for colours that I haven't had yet,' he told thoughtcatalog.com. 'I'm just going through the colour wheel and checking out what I haven't done. Now I'm going to have to start to do patterns.'

The guys have stated on many occasions that they are all simply too busy with their 5SOS commitments to have a serious relationship, but that hasn't stopped Mike forming at least three friendship crushes. The main one is the Grammy Award winner Bruno

'We went to bed and when we woke up Mike had an eyebrow piercing. It must have been midnight and he went out on his own and came back the next morning with an eyebrow piercing.'

Luke

Mars, because he 'would just be badass to be friends with . . . I feel like he'd be really nice.' The others are reggae legend Bob Marley and the actor Jack Black – possibly owing to Mike being appreciative of Jack's own fretwork in *Tenacious D: the Pick of Destiny* and *School of Rock*.

Mike is rather more reticent when it comes to naming his actual crushes, although he has admitted to an online flirtation with Camila Cabello from the American girl band, Fifth Harmony. He also playfully told the *Hollywood Life* website that he would definitely marry Miley Cyrus, before quickly retracting his comment on the grounds that, 'Miley wasn't ready for marriage'.

As a guitarist in *the* band of the moment, Mike isn't short of female admirers. He did date a few girls at Norwest, but unlike with Luke and Aleisha, none of his crushes developed into anything meaningful – at least not for him . . .

On being asked to describe his dream girl during an interview with *Top of the Pops* magazine, Mike said she'd have to be funny, weird and caring. 'I don't know if I've met her yet,' he continued. 'But then maybe I have and just haven't known it.'

Live on Today, Mike pays tribute to American Idiot by Green Day – one of his all-time favourite albums.

Chapter Three

Unplugged and Unfazed

'You've got to be conscious about what you want people to know about your personal lives, but we like to share a lot. If you're in a band, you can't be that rock-star type of dude who no one knows about and you're all mysterious. The fans want to know you.'

Ash

With the three-city mini tour looming large, 5 Seconds of Summer posted their first ever original song on YouTube, the aptly named 'Gotta Get Out'. Every member of the 5SOS Family (the name coined by Ash to describe the band's ever-growing army of adoring fans; 'we thought, "why don't we just call them family?"' the drumming cutie explained via Facebook, amidst many pink heart emoticons) will remember the date when this handsome new video appeared: 21 May 2012. Filled with gorgeous close-ups of each of the guys in turn, the polished clip was a cut above anything that 5SOS had posted before.

Though slower in tempo than some of the rocking riffs the guys were rehearsing behind the scenes, 'Gotta Get Out' bounces along with a lilting beat and the boys' voices soaring in highly-infectious harmony – all of which would soon become a 5SOS hallmark. The song was written by Cal while he was still finding his way around the bass guitar. Though it is the first original track he ever wrote, the bittersweet lyrics – swinging between love and heartbreak, hope and despair – show a maturity way beyond his years.

While 5SOS have always been social-media savvy, fans were delighted to see their online activity go into overdrive in the days leading up to their two sell-out shows at Sydney Factory Theatre. Aside from cranking up the excitement with a countdown to show-time, the guys launched a fan-art competition whereby the best entrants not only received an exclusive merchandising pack, but could also get up close and personal with Luke, Mike, Cal and Ash at special meet-and-greet sessions staged at each venue before the show.

All about the 5SOSFam: backstage at a HMV signing for She Looks So Perfect *(left) and outside Z100 Studio in New York (below), April 2014.*

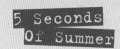

Fortunately for the 5SOS Family, moody mystique has never been the boys' style. Unlike other more private pop-rockers, 5SOS have made every effort to stay close to their fanbase, making them feel connected every step of the way. Hence, daily tweets, goofy backstage gatherings and Instagram pics aplenty are still very much on the agenda for Cal, Luke, Ash and Mike. 'It's not the eighties anymore,' Ash said pointedly. 'We're not a mysterious rock star. People know everything we do.'

Though grounded 5SOS may still not see themselves as rock stars, the rapturous welcome they received in both Brisbane and Melbourne would suggest otherwise. In both cities, girls turned out in their thousands – all hoping to catch a glimpse of the gorgeous rockers. Brisbane Airport bosses called in extra security for the occasion, while 5SOS themselves were forced to spend the hours before the show holed up in their hotel room. Looking out from said room – across the horde of fans gathered down in the street – was undoubtedly a surreal experience for the boys, especially Luke who was desperately trying to cram for a maths exam the following Monday.

> 'We spend a lot of time on social media . . . we have our own individual Twitters, we have the main band Twitter and our Facebook accounts, and that's going crazy.'
>
> **Calum**

Similar scenes awaited them in Melbourne, of course. Since Luke, Cal, Ash and Mike were local boys, the *Sydney Morning Herald* had been keeping a watchful eye on 5SOS's progress from wannabes to must-sees. The paper had reported on the mini-tour and upon the boys' return to Sydney at the end of June, entertainment reporter Toby Creswell caught up with them at their compact rehearsal space, located within an industrial park on Sydney's north-western fringe.

As if striving for straight As while remembering to switch from A to A# on the final chorus of 'Out Of My Limit' was not taxing enough, the *Herald* discovered the guys' working day didn't end with the ninety-minute drive back to Riverstone after rehearsals. Such is 5SOS's dedication to their fans – and keeping them up-to-date with everything in their world – that they each spent a couple of hours on Twitter and Facebook before calling it a night. 'We spend a lot of time on [social media],' Cal explained. 'We have our own individual Twitters; we have the main band Twitter and our Facebook accounts – and that's going crazy.'

'I went from 300 Facebook friends to 5,000 and 8,000 subscribers almost overnight,' Ash added. 'We pay attention to our online fans and they really give it back. They share our stuff and they are really coming on the journey with us. It's one of the important elements of what we do.'

'We're on Twitter and Facebook all the time,' he continued, 'keeping fans updated on YouTube, and constantly releasing things to keep them knowing we're putting the effort in.'

This wasn't the only slightly surreal change that the boys were noticing. 'Having people notice you in the street – that's weird,' Mike said. 'We went to McDonald's the other day and sat in the corner and every single person in [there] knew who we were. And I found out later that, after we'd left, this group of girls sat in the spot we were sitting at and, like, smelt it!'

Sadly, not all 5SOS's experiences as four of the hottest rising stars in rock have been positive. Not everything that twitters is gold, after all . . . and Cal, Ash, Mike and Luke have all come in

Hottie in a hood: Calum stops to greet a group of devoted fans outside Z100 Studios.

for a certain amount of online hate. Rather than ignore the trolls, Ash decided to face these twisted Twitter-users head on.

'Be with us or against us,' he tweeted. 'Don't like what we are doing, it's fine, this is the real s**t, all for the fans, don't dare tell me otherwise.' In another tweet he defiantly proclaimed: 'A heart that hurts is a heart that works.'

To capitalise on the growing 5SOS groundswell, the guys unveiled plans for the Twenty Twelve Tour. Scheduled to run from late July to early August, this tour again comprised dates in Sydney, Brisbane, and Melbourne, as well as an additional show in Adelaide.

The Sydney and Brisbane shows sold out almost before the ink was dry on the tickets and the other dates weren't far behind.

★★★★

Around this time, 5 Seconds of Summer took to Facebook to announce some particularly special news . . . the impending release of their first EP, *Unplugged*, via iTunes on 26 July. It was, perhaps, the most monumental milestone in the band's career to date. Due to unforeseen circumstances, the original release date had to be postponed for a week. To compensate for the disappointing news, the guys playfully wove the delayed release date into a fanciful tale about Mount Everest, a bear and their having to send Cal off to Nepal to retrieve the EP. It's a wonder they didn't say Ash was the one who'd scaled Everest as punishment for his believing 'EP' stood for 'Episode', rather than 'Extended Play'.

Of the four acoustic tracks on the EP, two were original 5SOS compositions – 'Gotta Get Out' and 'Too Late' – while the remaining tracks were covers of Blink-182's 'I Miss You' and All Time Low's 'Jasey Rae', (the latter of which appeared on *Punk Goes Acoustic 2* in 2007).

With no professional marketing team to publicise the EP for them, it was left to the guys themselves to spread the word about their upcoming release. The DIY promotion campaign included a week-long trawl of interviews, meet-and-greet signing sessions, Ustream chats and a thrilling unplugged performance live on Nova FM.

Clearly, 5SOS's hard graft paid off, with the EP peaking at number three on the Australian iTunes chart, as well as creeping into the Top 20 in the official Australian and New Zealand charts. The EP also caught the imagination of teenagers in Sweden, where it scored the guys another top-three hit on iTunes.

As debut releases go, *Unplugged* was an unqualified success and – with the incredible demand for tickets to the Twenty Twelve Tour – this EP was obviously the work of a band ready to expand their horizons well beyond Australia.

Or was it? The tours and EP were all part of Adam Wilkinson and Matt Emsell's master-plan for 5SOS, but even they weren't wholly convinced that their four teen artists were ready

'We were saying that hopefully we are just going to be able to walk through the middle of everyone and no one will care. I don't think that will be the case now.'

Mike

to transition from local heroes to global stars. Little could they have known that, halfway across the world, fate was taking a hand in their story . . .

On receiving reports about an Australian band that had amassed a 50,000-strong following on Facebook, were releasing their own music and playing sell-out tours, One Direction's Louis Tomlinson went online to see for himself what all the 5SOS fuss was about. According to 5SOS legend, the band's Facebook page led Louis to Luke's YouTube account. He was particularly impressed by the 'Teenage Dirtbag' video, and there was something about 5 Seconds of Summer's obvious charm that suggested they might make the perfect support act for One Direction's mammoth Take Me Home world tour that was set to get underway the following summer.

By the time Adam Wilkinson and Matt Emsell were trading transpacific phone calls with their opposite numbers at One Direction's own representatives at Modest Management, the guys were out on the road on the Twenty Twelve Tour.

Speaking with *Punktastic* in March 2014, Cal recalled the band's collective shock on hearing that they'd been singled out by One Direction. 'In Adelaide, we were having lunch and we had this piece of paper that was put in front of us telling us we were doing a world tour and listing all the venues. It was just an endless piece of paper – mind-blowing!'

Hooked on 5SOS's infectious riffs, the UK boyband had specifically requested their presence on the UK, North American, and Australasian legs of their upcoming world tour. The news didn't initially sit well with everyone, however, as Ash revealed live on ITV's breakfast show,

'X Factor': Mikey gets into the zone, live onstage at the Royal Oak Music Theatre, Michigan, April 2014.

This Morning, in June 2014. 'That opportunity came and we were unsure because we're nothing like One Direction and it wasn't the type of thing we were going for.'

Ash would, of course, subsequently rethink his stance, because as Cal said, traversing the UK and America performing in stadiums and arenas in front of sell-out crowds was going to be a 'mind-blowing' experience – especially as the Australasian leg of the tour included six sell-out shows at Sydney's 21,000-capacity Allphones Arena.

Once the euphoria wore off, 5SOS realised they were going to need to get their song-writing heads on. Opening for One Direction was a crucial chance for them to introduce their sound to teens around the world – they weren't about to let it go to waste. Adam Wilkinson and Matt Emsell's long-term strategy for 5 Seconds of Summer had always been to release an EP featuring original material only – this would be the platform for 5SOS's first full-length album.

The get-togethers with Christian Lo Russo and Joel Chapman had proved extremely productive in terms of filtering ideas and helping the guys clarify what musical direction was right for them. For, while their shared love of pop punk is what brought Luke, Mike, Cal and Ash together, to have slavishly imitated their heroes – Green Day, Good Charlotte, Blink-182 et al. – would not have been enough for any of the boys. Despite the contents of their iPods, 5SOS knew they needed to find a voice of their own.

Diversifying their repertoire to include mid- and even slow-tempo numbers was also part of the revised strategy as the vast majority of up-and-coming pop-punk bands – as featured in the pages of *Kerrang!* magazine – tended to play every song at breakneck pace. 'If there's one thing I

Homecoming king: Ash prepares to play a show at Martin Place, Sydney, May 2014.

hate about pop-punk, it's people thinking you have to do the whole [double-time] thing,' Ash told *Alternative Press*. 'I think it's a bit ugly. I was raised on that. When I'd go to pubs and see bands like that, I'd just think, "Slow down!"'

One thing that wouldn't be slowing down any time soon, of course, was the 5SOS express. Instead of relying solely on Christian Lo Russo and Joel Chapman, Adam Wilkinson and Matt Emsell put out extended feelers to see who else might be interested in collaborating with Luke, Mike, Cal and Ash. The response to what were, after all, tentative entreaties was more than they could ever have hoped for.

Negotiations over 5 Seconds of Summer supporting One Direction on the Take Me Home tour were still ongoing, and therefore very hush-hush, and yet proven song-writing luminaries such as Kaiser Chiefs' Nick Hodgson, Tom Fletcher of McFly, and Busted duo, Steve Robson and James Bourne, were all expressing their interest in working with this hot new band from Australia.

5 Seconds of Summer were scheduled to play a free open-air show in Sydney's Hyde Park at the end of August, after which they had a month-long window before going out on the road with Hot Chelle Rae on the Australian leg of the US rock outfit's Whatever world tour. So it was that, in late September, the guys packed their travel bags and headed for London on a two-week song-writing trip.

Aside from getting together with Nick Hodgson, Tom Fletcher, Steve Robson and James Bourne, the guys sent out notices via Facebook and Twitter inviting their British fans along to another free open-air show in Hyde Park. Australia may have been in the grip of 5SOS fever, but the size of the boys' UK audience was still a relative unknown . . . and so, the Hyde Park date was something of a gamble that could have ended in humiliation had no one bothered to show on the day.

Thankfully, their blushes were spared by the fifty or so 5SOSers who turned up to hear to the guys play a short set. These same lucky girls were also treated to a chat with the Aussie foursome afterwards. One obvious topic of conversation would have been 5 Seconds of Summer's future plans for touring the UK. The guys knew that if everything went according to plan they'd be opening for One Direction, but were, of course, sworn to secrecy . . .

Luke, Mike, Cal and Ash returned home to Sydney fully invigorated by their first 5SOS assignment overseas – and ready to knuckle down to some serious rehearsals in preparation for the opening date of the Hot Chelle Rae tour at Sydney's Enmore Theatre on 22 October.

Speaking with *Hot Hits* two shows in, Ash admitted to it being 'pretty scary' owing to the tour being the 'biggest . . . we've done so far.'

Mikey, for his part, described the whole experience as 'amazing'. Of his tourmates in Hot Chelle Rae, he had nothing but the kindest things to say. '[They] were really down to earth . . . nicer than I thought they were going to be,' he revealed. Quizzed as to how the support slot had come about, he began joking that there was a 'conspiracy' surrounding the invite. In fact Chelle's

> 'We pay attention to our online fans and they really give it back. They share our stuff and they are really coming on the journey with us. It's one of the important elements of what we do.'
> Ash

'Tonight Tonight' has always been one of 5SOS's favourite covers; someone saw them playing the song, liked what they heard and reported back to the Nashville trio . . .

Following on from the final Hot Chelle Rae date at Perth's Astor Theatre on 1 November, the guys flew over to New Zealand for a show at the Zeal Global Café in Auckland; their first ever paid gig overseas.

They had been hoping to meet up with One Direction whilst they were in London. Not only so that they might thank Louis Tomlinson in person for championing them for the Take Me Home tour, but also to see if they were any nearer to getting official confirmation that they were booked onto the tour. The opportunity hadn't presented itself, but if the guys were getting anxious then they needn't have worried because three days after the Auckland show, Louis tipped them the unofficial wink via his Twitter account. 'Been a fan of this band for a while, everyone get behind them,' he tweeted along with a link to 'Gotta Get Out' on YouTube. Within a matter of days some 75,000 Directioners had watched and retweeted the video.

The 5SOS Facebook page also received plenty of attention in the wake of Louis' tweet. Although the guys were under strict instruction from Adam Wilkinson and Matt Emsell to keep the Take Me Home tour support slot under wraps until the contract was signed, sealed and delivered, they were able to announce to Facebook friends old and new that they'd worked up a rockier version of 'Gotta Get Out' for inclusion on their *Somewhere New* EP, which was set for release the first week in December.

To promote the new EP, the guys released the video to 'Out of my Limit' as a separate digital download. Within days the video had received over 100,000 hits - one of which came from Louis Tomlinson's fellow 1Der, Niall Horan, who raved: 'Just been showed this video - TUNNNEEEEE!'

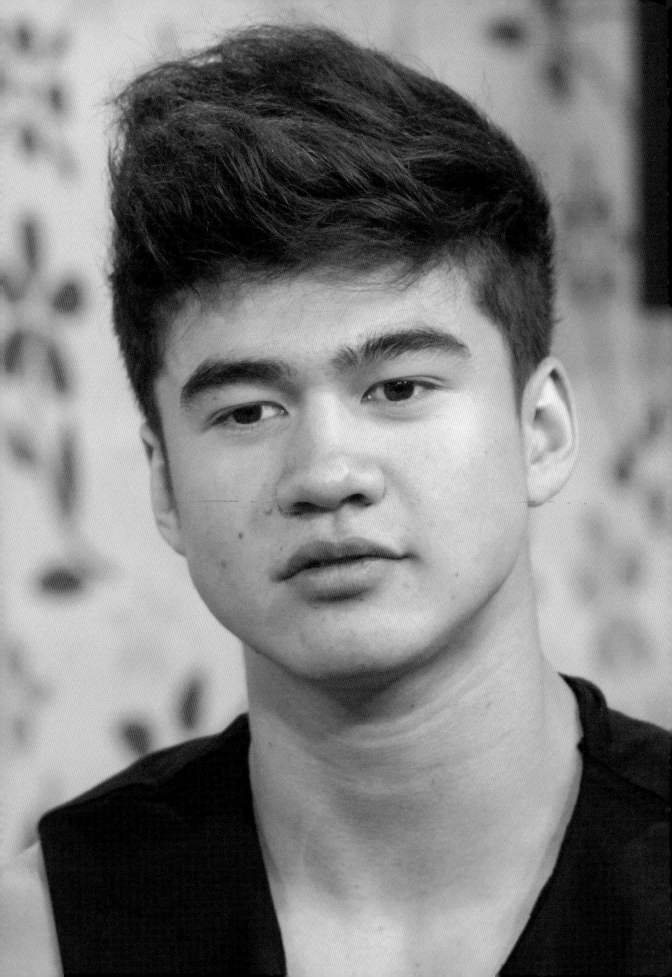

Calum Hood Fact File

Birth Date: 25 January 1996

Star sign: Aquarius

Secret SOS: 'One thing nobody knows about me? I probably squat on a daily basis.'

Words to live by: 'Just live right now, and be yourself, it doesn't matter if it's good enough for someone else.'

Calum Thomas Hood was born on 25 January 1996. Like Luke and Michael, he grew up in Riverstone, Western Sydney, and attended Norwest Christian College. While his Christian name stems from his father David's Scottish ancestry, he undoubtedly gets his sultry Maori looks from his mum, New Zealand-born Joy.

Calum is an Aquarian, ruled by the planet Neptune, all of which explains his happy-go-lucky temperament – a trait of Cal's that helps him get along with most people and which we've grown to love. Ash once joked that we have Cal to thank for the fact that 5SOS are together today, saying that the bassist 'romanced' him via eHarmony until he agreed to sign up. Sadly, Cal is not to be found on eHarmony . . . but even so, there's more than a grain of truth in Ash's story. In fact, sunny Cal is the mutual friend who helped Luke and Michael stop hating each other. He was also the first 5SOS member to properly bond with drummer Ash. Cadging regular lifts to band practice (even back then, Ash had a car) was an excellent excuse for Cal to break the ice with 5SOS's new recruit.

Given his Celtic-Maori roots and the fact that he was raised in rugby-mad Australia, one

Cal's sultry appearance on This Morning *inspired many 5SOSers to get out of bed, June 2014.*

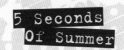

might have expected Calum to show a flair for the sport. Yet his talent – and interest – lay in a different-shaped ball. Actively encouraged by his dad, who would join him for regular kick-abouts in the garden or down the local park, Calum began to show genuine ability in 'soccer' (the Australian name for football) – so much so that he ended up being selected for a schoolboys' XI to represent his country in a competition in Brazil, the so-called 'home of football'.

The Australian team may not rank so highly in the FIFA ratings, but few sporty teens would turn down the chance of a career as a world-class footballer. And Calum might well have followed in the footsteps of Aussie sports stars Harry Kewell, Tim Cahill and Mark Schwarzer, by playing in the Premier League had making music with Luke and Michael not distracted him (quite literally) from his goal. He still has a pair of football boots and dusts them off for the occasional game 'every now and then'. Moving to England with his 5SOS bandmates has also allowed him to watch his beloved Liverpool FC – the team he's supported since childhood – in the flesh rather than on TV.

> *'I like a girl who's quirky, funny and slightly weird. We're weird guys so it needs to be balanced out.'*
>
> Calum

Given what he has gone on to achieve with 5SOS, Calum clearly made the right decision in choosing four strings over soccer, but he isn't the only member of the Hood clan with a musical bent. In 2012, his elder sister, Mali-Koa, appeared on *The Voice – Australia*. The then twenty-year-old wowed the judges in the blind-auditions round (episode four) with her rendition of 'American Boy' by Estelle, before being knocked out at the 'battle' stage. Her mentor on the show was Good Charlotte's Joel Madden and, while 5SOS would subsequently collaborate with Joel, the boys probably pestered poor Mali to death for behind-the-scenes anecdotes about their idol.

This was far from the end of Mali's career and the songstress still performs regularly in and around Sydney. Thanks to the exposure she gained through appearing on *The Voice* – not to mention her kid brother being in the then rapidly up-and-coming 5 Seconds of Summer – Mali was asked to serve as a head judge on the 2012 series of a local TV talent show, *The Hills Are Alive*. In a show of support, Calum went along to the studio to watch the series finale and even got up onstage with Mali to perform Chris Brown's 'Forever' and Katy Perry's 2010 US chart-topper, 'Teenage Dream,' which has, of course, since become a crowd-pleasing 5SOS cover song.

It was Mali who unwittingly set Calum on his own future career path. 'When I was younger, my sister was a big fan of R&B – Usher and Chris Brown,' he said. 'I got a lot of my love for R&B from her. She used to sing all the time, and I used to wonder why I wasn't as good as her.'

Calum has a tattoo of a bird with 'Mali-Koa' written underneath. 'She's my best friend and no one else gets me like she does,' he said in a recent interview. 'I go to her for everything.'

He also has a tattoo bearing his parents' initials. In this way, he feels they're with him wherever he goes. 'It brings me good luck,' he said. 'Family is everything.'

It was, of course, Chris Brown's 'Next To You' that proved the catalyst for Calum, Luke and Michael's subsequent 5SOS success. When the boys were invited to attend the MTV Video Music Awards at the Forum in LA in August 2014, Calum admitted he'd been frantically learning his lines should he find himself rubbing shoulders with the controversial rapper.

Calum is 5SOS's most prodigious songwriter. He has seven co-writing credits on the

Crazy for Cal: 5SOS's cheekiest member greets his public outside of the Billboard Music Awards, May 2014.

debut album and is responsible for a string of bonus tracks besides. Excitingly, he's written many more songs that, as yet, remain unrecorded. And it appears that he has a very famous forebear to thank for his lyrical wizardry, because in October 2014 he stunned the Twittersphere by revealing that he could be the fourteenth grandson twice removed of William Shakespeare. To legitimise his connection with the illustrious bard, he shared a poem that he wrote aged six about a turtle that 'lived in side a big, big cave,' and was 'smalla then a bug'. The end of the story is unexpectedly violent, telling how the tiny creature 'lade' an egg with a 'bom' on it that 'blowd up'.

Even Calum is prone to occasional bouts of writer's block, however. 'I spend a lot of time on it,' he told the *Sydney Morning Herald*. 'Some days it doesn't come, and I'm angry the whole night.'

Although he can't possibly regulate when and where the ideas will flow, Calum has disciplined himself to avoid writing while out on the road. 'I'm a strong believer in going out on the road and focusing on touring and living life a bit,' he told *Alter the Press*. 'It kind of gives you fuel to write when you're back in the studio.'

The sound of 5SOS may be pop-punk, but Calum has admitted to having an eclectic taste in music. Speaking on the *Hot 30* twitcam, he named his favourite singer as Guy Sebastian, winner of the first series of *Australian Idol*, while other standouts on his iPod are American rockers Boys like Girls, Chris Brown and Nicki Minaj.

'I'm a strong believer in going out on the road and focusing on touring and living life a bit. It kind of gives you fuel to write when you're back in the studio.'

Calum

Calum Hood

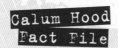
Like the rest of 5SOS, Calum is a 'big Katy Perry fan,' but his appreciation extends beyond Katy's music as he's singled out the Santa Barbara babe as the 'person he'd most like to be stuck in a lift with'. Another celebrity crush with whom Calum would like to make sweet music is Aussie singer-songwriter, Delta Goodrem, whose 2003 album, *Innocent Eyes*, sold four million copies around the world. But the delectable Delta isn't the only home-grown girl to hold a place in Calum's heart. Cal recently joked that he's still crushing on his year two teacher, Miss Willis. 'It's been twelve years,' he laughed. He's also playfully confessed having a 'man crush' on Kellin Quinn, saying that he would 'turn gay' for the Sleeping with Sirens frontman.

With 5SOS's touring and recording commitments showing no sign of slowing up any time soon, Calum, like the rest of the band, has precious little time for girls and is not looking to get into a relationship any time soon. He does, however, know what type he's looking for in future. 'I like a girl who's quirky, funny and slightly weird,' he told *Top of the Pops* magazine. 'We're weird guys so it needs to be balanced out.'

Speaking with *Seventeen* magazine, Calum described himself as 'the chill dude,' but he certainly sent many a female pulse soaring when a five-second Snapchat video of him teasingly revealing 'little Calum' was leaked online.

Snapchat videos and images are automatically deleted, but unfortunately for Calum, his unnamed female acquaintance was filming him on a separate phone and subsequently uploaded the video to Vine, with the caption: 'CALUMS D*** IM SCREAMING'.

Though Calum was careful to keep his head out of the shot, the video quickly went viral. Rather than deny it was him, Cal decided to come clean via Twitter. 'Least ya know what it looks like now,' he posted. And to nip any social-media backlash in the bud, he later offered an apology of sorts, saying: 'I'm still just a teenage kid learning from mistakes.'

This of course wasn't the first time Calum had sent his fans into an online frenzy, as a Snapchat photo of him cooking breakfast with his back to the camera, wearing nothing but a beanie, and another in which he is facing the camera with only a baseball cap to cover his modesty, had already done the rounds online.

When quizzed about these photos during an interview on *Sunrise* in September 2014, Calum again seized the initiative. 'I'm proud of that,' he stated simply. In the same interview, his bandmates also made light of the so-called 'below the belt scandal'. Cal's 'shameless habit of stripping down' is common knowledge to Luke, Michael and Ash, who've all seen his 'naked butt' hundreds of times.

Luke told *Seventeen* that, in their shared flat in London, he'd come downstairs and caught Calum making a cup of tea naked. Naturally, he took a photo – 'Calum's butt is everywhere now,' he said.

Fans would get another eyeful of Cal's behind later that same month when the band uploaded a saucy Snapchat from rehearsal showing the unabashed bassist with his back to the camera, naked from the ankles up. Just because Calum was happy to be snapped in the buff whilst rustling up breakfast didn't necessarily mean he knew his way around a kitchen. In an interview with Pressparty.com, he confessed that he still has to rely on home for cooking tips. 'I still text my mum everyday, like "how do you cook pasta?" because I still don't know ...!'

Irresistible ink: Cal plays in 5SOS's private show at Radio Y-100, Miami, October 2014.

Chapter Four

Gotta Get Out (There)

'We discovered 5SOS on YouTube last year and we all knew
straightaway they were very special. We're so excited
to have them on the road with us and we know our
fans are going to love what these lads do.'

Niall Horan

Even after two exceptionally public shout-outs from Louis and Niall – whose tweets inspired a frenzy of online interest in the band – 5 Seconds of Summer were still yet to be officially revealed as One Direction's support act of choice for the Take Me Home world tour. Whilst waiting for the news to break, the boys could barely contain their excitement. The same was true for their management team, the professionals they'd worked with in the studio and, of course, the families still rooting for them back home.

Yet for the 5SOS parents, the excitement was tempered by concerns for the future of their sons. Heading out on the road with 1D would mean dropping out of full-time education indefinitely. 5SOS's concerned parents wanted to be sure that Luke, Cal, Ash and Mike would not live to regret so drastic a step. To be attended by approximately 1.3 million besotted fans, the 107 shows that 5SOS were scheduled to play with 1D would bring them exposure beyond their wildest dreams. Yet nothing is for certain in the fickle music industry – even for an act being championed by One Direction. Whether 5 Seconds of Summer would last longer than the Take Me Home tour was anyone's guess . . .

Adam Wilkinson was new to music management, but Matt Emsell had undoubtedly dealt with his share of anxious parents before. Aside from the obvious financial benefits, he could have pointed out the hugely promising facts of the situation: One Direction had expressly requested 5 Seconds of Summer as their opening act. Not only that but, whereas Justice Crew

Left: 5SOS strike a typically sassy pose in London, July 2014. Below: rehearsing for their hyper-charged set at the 2014 Billboard Music Awards.

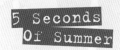

and Johnny Ruffo – the last Australian acts to be chosen for the prestigious opening slot on 1D's Up All Night tour – had only played with One Direction in their home country, 5SOS would be a fixture for the duration of 1D's time in the UK and North America as well as Oz.

Fortunately for the boys – and 5SOSers everywhere in the world – Emsell was eventually able to talk their parents round. Their sons were in this for the long haul, after all, and determined to follow their dreams. 'They had faith for some reason,' Ash said later, 'and they really got behind it in the end.'

Indeed, such was Liz Hemmings' devotion to 5SOS that she even ended up accompanying the band on part of the UK leg of the Where We Are tour a couple of years down the line in 2014. In an interview with Radio Nova in May 2014 (on which she was a surprise phone-guest – much to Luke's embarrassment as he and Mikey had just confessed to sneaking away from hotels without settling their respective mini-bar bills) Liz said that the guys had become 'self-sufficient' pretty quickly and that she'd only had to adopt a motherly tone early on to ensure that they 'eat a proper breakfast'.

> '**I guess you can't really rehearse for stadiums. You have to just be thrown into the deep end and go from there.**'
>
> Calum

★★★★

The opening date of the UK leg of the Take Me Home tour was at London's O2 Arena on 23 February 2013 and now that the boys had their families backing them 100 percent, they decided on an extended foray to London where they could prepare for the tour free from distractions. And following a show at Sydney's Metro Theatre, which had been originally booked to promote the *Somewhere New* EP, but now served as a farewell to their hometown fans, the boys were on their way.

No sooner had they stocked the kitchen cupboards in the two-storey flat that would serve as their base-camp until the end of April, than they booked time at Nick Hodgson's East London recording studio, Chewdio. Hodgson had quit Kaiser Chiefs on 5 December – coincidently, the same day the boys arrived in London – to concentrate on making a name for himself in the production world. Hence, 5SOS were a welcome first project.

In between their sessions at Chewdio, the boys worked with a host of other songwriters including: Roy Stride from Scouting for Girls; Rick Parkhouse and George Tizzard – a hit-making duo who'd worked for Little Mix and Cheryl Cole amongst others and Richard 'Biff' Stannard, whose Brighton-based production company Biffco had already clocked up forty-one chart hits (including nine number ones) and had scooped an Ivor Novello Award for the Spice Girls' breakthrough single, 'Wannabe'.

5SOS also spent a significant amount of time with Steve Robson, the multi-instrumentalist and producer who'd written songs for a host of acts including Take That, One Direction and Busted, and would, of course, collaborate with Luke and Calum on 'Don't Stop' during the London sessions. Since Robson is credited as a huge influence on the sound of Busted – an Essex-based trio who, in turn, shaped Michael's style of playing – working with 5SOS felt like

Boys on tour: Mike and Cal get the party started, opening for One Direction at the Met Life Stadium – on the Brit boys' Where We Are tour, 4 August 2014.

coming full circle. Michael, for one, was thrilled just to be in the same room as his idol. 'It's pretty cool to work with people whose music you have listened to and loved,' he told the *Daily Telegraph*. '[Steve's] done heaps so that was a pretty big deal. I have asked him for a bunch of stories because he did Busted, and they are one of my favourite bands . . . he was the coolest dude.'

As to the question of who would be supporting One Direction on the Take Me Home tour, the world's media was still in the dark, but with Luke, Michael, Calum and Ash now spending more and more time with the boys from 1D, it is surprising none of the UK tabloids sniffed out what was going under their noses.

Niall was the first to drop by Chewdio to introduce himself and to hang out with the boys, but it wasn't long before Louis, Liam, Zayn and Harry followed suit. 'They're just normal people, to be honest,' Ash later said about the ongoing bromance. 'They're nice boys to hang out with and we don't have many friends over here.'

During one of their Chewdio visits, Niall and co. challenged 5SOS to a game of footie. Given the fifteen – two score-line it's obvious 1D didn't give the Aussie boys any quarter.

'We got absolutely demolished,' Michael told news.com.au. 'They turned up with all this gear and we thought we were just going to hang out and kick the ball around but they were serious. Maybe we could challenge them on rugby.'

The drubbing must have been especially embarrassing for the Liverpool FC-loving Calum, seeing as he once represented Australia in the sport. Before hanging up his boots in favour of bass, he even harboured dreams of becoming a professional footballer.

5SOS were well aware that their international fan base was still largely made up of One Direction fans, girls who had latched onto them through Louis' and Niall's tweets. Yet these

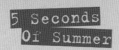
same Directioners would have been surprised to learn that, while they were hugely flattered at being invited on the tour, Luke, Michael, Calum and Ash were all initially reticent to accept. They could guess the kind of comparisons that the pairing would bring and were anxious not to be written off as 'just another manufactured boyband' before they'd even started out.

Speaking with the *Sun* shortly after the tour's opening date, Luke explained, 'We looked up to the likes of Blink-182 and Green Day, so we felt that it would be kind of weird for us and we didn't know what to do. We thought [1D] were cool, but we did look at them as a pop band and we didn't want to be that. But then we met the boys and thought they were awesome.'

They were also understandably apprehensive at what appeared to be – back then at least – a

> 'We're not trying to be anything we're not. We're not the new anything. We're the first 5 Seconds of Summer.'
>
> Luke

once-in-a-lifetime offer. And who could blame them? For a fledgling band of pop-rockers, it was almost too amazing an opportunity to be believed. They were still getting to grips with appearing in front of two or three thousand people; on tour with 1D, they'd be playing to ten times that number.

In an attempt to establish their credentials, the boys staged a series of busking and meet-and-greet events in and around London in the lead-up to the opening O2 date. Despite their efforts, it's fair to say that the average British One Direction fan was probably expecting 5 Seconds of Summer to be yet another wannabe boyband harbouring questionable intentions of stealing their idols' crown.

★★★★

On Valentine's 2013, 5SOS were finally able to share their 'pretty BIG news' with the 5SOSFam. But rather than simply put it out there, they did so in typical 5SOS style, via a heartfelt post on Facebook:

HOW THE HELL AND WHY ARE WE GOING ON THE 1D TOUR? Well a little while ago a lad by the name of Louis Tomlinson stumbled across a video of ours on YouTube, and long story short he showed the rest of the guys and they really liked what we were doing. One Direction wanted a band to come on tour with them! And well, we are a band and it's so cool that we are what they wanted! We have known for a little while but have not been allowed to tell anyone until today. We have been so desperate to tell you. But now we can't wait to show the world our tunes! And we cannot wait to make you all proud! To the incredibly dedicated and amazing fans that have been here from the start and the amazing fans that support us now. This is a journey we all are going on, not just us boys in the band, but all of you! Really looking forward for this next year. We love you guys sooooo much and cant wait to hopefully play in your country and you can come and watch us! thank you all again we appreciate every little thing you do for us. thank you!!
– mikey, ashton, luke & cal. xxxx

Hot SOS: Ash and Luke rock out at the 2014 Billboard Music Awards.

*Love is . . . Cal onstage at the iHeartRadio Music Festival,
September 2014.*

Needless to say, the announcement propelled 5 Seconds of Summer into the spotlight. Of course, 5SOS knew their real fans wouldn't see them hooking up with One Direction as selling out, but they were all too ready to defend themselves against those who might. 'Ask any bar band, "Would you rather go from [what they're doing] to flying first-class and staying in nice hotels?"' Michael asked defiantly. 'I guarantee every single one of them would say, "Hell yeah!"'

They further qualified their decision during an interview with *60 Minutes*. 'By them taking us on tour, it's given us the chance to show their audience a rockier side of pop,' Ash said. 'We're not a boyband – we're a band. We don't want to be called the next One Direction. That's not us.'

'A lot of bands have to change what they sound like, but we are exactly the band that we want to be: a pop band definitely, but we've got a rock and punk edge,' Luke added. 'We're not trying to be anything we're not. We're not the new anything. We're the first 5 Seconds of Summer.'

With 5SOS set to play six sell-out shows at the Allphones Arena in October 2013, the *Sydney Morning Herald* was keen to hear the band's thoughts and arranged a Skype call straight to their London hideaway.

'People were already calling us the new One Direction in Australia,' Luke said. 'But in our minds we're a lot different from them. We play guitars. We're rockier. But we thought that if you put us right next to each other, it would actually show how different we are.'

'We would not have done the One Direction tour if they wanted a boyband,' Ash added. 'The contrast between our bands is so huge, and that's what they [One Direction] wanted too.'

He also made it plain that the tour wouldn't distract them from their original goals. 'We're very focused on what we need to get done and how hard we do need to work,' Ash said. 'We're very self-motivated. We had to "take it to the next level" like five times in the last year.'

★★★★

In 5SOS's first interview with the *Sydney Morning Herald* (on the back of the Twenty Twelve tour), Calum told how stage-fright was keeping him awake at night. Back then, the crowds consisted of just 3,000 devoted 5SOSers. Now, he was faced with the prospect of playing to 20,000 Directioners, he had genuine cause for sleepless nights. Luke, Michael and Ash were no doubt equally anxious at the thought of stepping out onto the O2 stage. And although they now had five good friends close to hand – all of whom could empathise with what they were going through – no amount of advice could have prepared them for the immense experience that was to come.

'I guess you can't really rehearse for stadiums,' Calum told *Fuse* magazine. 'You have to just be thrown into the deep end and go from there. We're really just mentally preparing for what's about to happen.'

Even after countless pep talks from Louis, Liam, Niall, Zayn and Harry, Calum confesses to having been utterly overwhelmed by the magnitude of his surroundings – so much so that he spent the entirety of 5SOS's first show at the London O2 rooted to the same spot.

Over on drums, Ash was similarly struggling to hold it together – and unsurprisingly so. For a rock'n'roll band to transition from playing empty cinemas to sold-out stadiums in less than eighteen months is anything but usual. 'The first time we played with [One Direction] we'd done maybe twenty shows . . . and suddenly we were playing arenas in front of thousands of people,' he told the HMV website. 'We literally went from playing to twelve people in pubs to that . . . I looked up at one point, to see 18,000 people, all of whom seemed to be into it. It was crazy!'

> 'It's a massive experience to actually be in a band and learn how to control a stadium.'
> Ash

Having started out jamming in a dusty garage, playing 20,000-capacity arenas was taking some adjusting to. 'It's a massive experience to actually be in a band and learn how to control a stadium,' Ash stated on a separate occasion. 'You look up to people all your life – like Billie Joe [Armstrong] from Green Day and Dave Grohl – and how they command a stadium and perform and put on an intimate show in such a huge place.'

Luke, Michael, Calum and Ash would be the first to admit their O2 debut was far from flawless, but with another 106 shows to go, they could only grow in confidence, becoming a little more polished with each performance. Fortunately, owning the stage – however sizeable – is something that comes naturally to the charismatic Aussie foursome, as they demonstrated during a break in the 1D tour when they played the O2 Islington Academy on 14 May. This show – their very first as a headlining act in London – proved they were no flash-in-the-pan. Even without the draw of One Direction, all 800 tickets sold out within two minutes of going on sale.

With a month-long break before the opening show of the Take Me Home tour's North American leg, the boys returned home to Sydney. However, rather than head straight for Bondi Beach after enjoying some long overdue downtime with their families (and no one would have blamed them if they had), the boys scheduled an intimate homecoming show at Sydney's Oxford Art Factory on 21 May, following it up with a five-date mini tour of Oz in early June.

'It's cool to come home,' Luke told the *Australian Daily Telegraph* shortly after touching down on home soil. 'We wouldn't be anywhere without our Sydney fans, or our Australian fans. Those twelve people who were at the first show we played – they're the reason we're here now.'

The comically-titled Pants Down tour got underway with another home-turf outing at the Metro Theatre on 2 June, before talking in shows in Brisbane, Adelaide, Melbourne and (for the first time ever) Perth.

Ashton Irwin
Fact File

Birth Date: 7 July 1994
Star sign: Cancer
Secret SOS: 'I enjoy vanilla scented candles. A lot.'
Words to live by: 'People aren't kind, you aren't perfect, they aren't perfect, no one is.'

Ashton Fletcher Irwin was born on 7 July 1994, in Windsor, a suburb not far from Riverstone and very close to Freeman's Reach, where Luke lived. His heritage is more exotic, however, with rumoured Irish and American relatives on one side of the family or other . . .

Like Luke, Ash's star sign is Cancer, which means he's also brimming with crab-like intelligence. Those born on the seventh of the seventh are said to be especially intuitive and inclined to act on their hunches, which may explain why Ash leapt at the chance to team up with Luke, Michael and Calum. Ruled by the astrological planet of Neptune, ambitious Ash will do everything within his power to reach the top of his chosen profession.

In an interview with *Rock Sound* Ash made a point of stressing that none of the 5SOS boys ever felt like they belonged in their respective hometowns. Growing up in the dull – and occasionally threatening – suburbs meant they'd been forced 'to build something for ourselves because we didn't want to be where we lived'. What Ash didn't say was that he'd perhaps had to 'build' a little harder than Luke, Michael and Calum . . .

'My parents split when I was younger and, being the oldest, I had to look after my sister,'

Rocking tousled curls and his trademark bandana,
Ash makes a sexy TV appearance on This Morning.

Who's that guy? Ash rocks his favourite Unknown Pleasures *shirt on a visit to NRJ Radio, Paris, April 2014.*

he told *Top of the Pops* magazine. 'So growing up, it was me, my mum (Anne Marie), and my younger sister (Lauren) – just the three of us until my brother (Harry) came along.' Though he didn't mention him in this particular interview, Ash also has a step-brother named Josh from his father's second marriage.

Ash wasn't the only member of the band to grow up without a father figure in the home; Michael's mum, Karen, is also a single mother. Unlike Mike, however, Ash had younger siblings to consider, meaning he was forced to grow up faster than most. Most teenagers take on part-time jobs as a way of gaining extra cash to spend on themselves, but with money a constant worry in the Irwin household, Ash selflessly handed whatever he earned over to his mum, Anne Marie.

Ash himself has acknowledged that growing up without a dad – being forced to step into the role of 'man-of-the-house' – is 'a difficult thing to overcome'. Even so, it's not been a purely 'bad' experience as far as the drummer is concerned. One positive outcome, of course, is the extra-special bond he enjoys with his mum. His commitments with 5 Seconds of Summer have taken him far from home. But no matter where he is in the world, Ash dutifully reports back to let Anne Marie know that he's okay. 'He texts me every day: "Love you, mama",' she told *60 Minutes*. 'You get that text message, even if it's 3 o'clock in the morning.'

Ash is the oldest member of 5SOS by about sixteen months. As you'd expect, he seems to have slipped into the role of responsible elder brother while out on the road and in

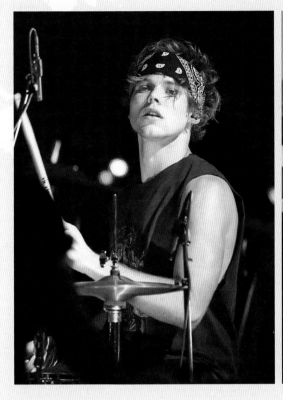 

Above left: banging the drums at the MTV Video Music Awards, August 2014. Right: deep in conversation with SiriusXM, April 2014.

their shared London pad. Serving as the band's unofficial spokesman, he tends to take the lead during group interviews.

He's also the only one in the band not to have attended Norwest Christian College. Instead he was educated at the non-Christian state school, Richmond High, in neighbouring Richmond. The logistical difficulties involved in getting Ash to Norwest and back again every day would probably have proved a deciding factor in Anne Marie's choice of school – even if she had been able to afford Norwest's astronomical yearly fees.

'My parents split when I was younger and, being the oldest, I had to look after my sister.'
Ash

Drums have clearly been Ash's passion from an early age – he got his first kit when he was just eight years old – but the multi-talented sticksman is also accomplished on piano, saxophone and guitar.

Despite getting knocked back from the 2010 series of *The X Factor Australia*, Ash's ambition never wavered. Musician was the only career he ever wanted and, on graduating from Richmond High, he signed up for a two-year TAFE (Technical and Further Education) music course at the Western Sydney Institute. Despite his obvious talent, however, things didn't go quite according to plan and he came away with a grade F.

Certain sections of the media were quick to seize on Michael's D in music, but Ash's

'Everybody thinks I'm a bit weird, but these boys like me and I like them, and we get along.'
Ash

Ashton Irwin

academic record made his bandmate look like a high achiever. Once the secret of Ash's 'big fat F' was out – exposed in a string of hurtful news stories – Ash suddenly found that all eyes were on him. Of course, the drummer remembers this a 'pretty sad moment' in his life, yet he wasn't the only one affected by the coverage. Incredibly – since Ash hadn't been trying to lay the blame on anyone but himself – when Ash logged onto his Facebook account shortly after the exposé, he found his former music teacher had inboxed him complaining that his comments had shown the WSI in an unfavourable light.

Despite his failure in the classroom, Ash was doing better out on the stage, making something of a name for himself on the Sydney rock scene playing drums with a variety of local outfits. While he was on the TAFE course he formed Swallow the Goldfish with his friend Blake Green. The venture would prove short-lived but – as outlined on the acoustic duo's Twitter page – they played original numbers as well as 'all your favourite songs of today's music'.

With English singer-songwriter James Morrison being Ash's favourite singer, one song in Swallow the Goldfish's repertoire should surely have been Morrison's 2006 debut single 'You Give Me Something' which was a top-ten hit in Australia.

As with Luke, Michael and Calum, Billie Joe and co. played a huge part in formulating Ash's thinking while growing up. 'It wasn't just their music that influenced me, it was the attitude behind it,' he said. 'When I was a kid, I sort of felt like it wasn't alright to be what I was. And they (Green Day) told me it was.'

On his official Twitter account Ash cites *Bullet in a Bible* (recorded live at Milton Keynes National Bowl on 19 June 2005) as his 'favourite recording in history [as it] helped me discover what I wanted to be in life . . . Rock out and entertain people.'

Ash may have discovered what he wanted to do in life, but he never imagined he'd be rocking out and entertaining people with Luke, Michael and Calum. He'd checked out their YouTube offerings and hadn't thought much of what he saw; the trio's worst sin in his eyes being forgetting the lyrics.

There must have been something about them he liked, however, or he never would have responded to Michael's Facebook message, inviting him to play the Annandale gig. Nor was he put out when all but a dozen or so of the promised 200 attendees failed to show. At least Anne Marie was there to cheer him on . . .

'I met these boys and everything felt okay,' he later explained. 'Everybody thinks I'm a bit weird, but these boys like me and I like them, and we get along.' Ash, of course, had only been invited to play that one show, and not actually join 5 Seconds of Summer, but this was soon rectified when Calum got down on one knee and proposed to him to be in the band. Ash accepted and – despite having a chronic fear of needles – he has since confirmed his commitment to 5 Seconds of Summer by having the 5SOS logo tattooed on his wrist.

While Luke and Mikey's coifs have seen them hailed as the band's main trendsetters, Ash has got his own 5SOS thing going as he's rarely seen, either on or off the stage, without one of his trademark bandanas.

Self-described 'man of 1,000 drumming faces,' Ash slows it down for a show at Radio Y-100, October 2014.

Chapter Five

Life in Different Colours

'Some people think, "Oh, they're just another boyband. They'll have a thing and then disappear". But we're challenging that thought. We're so proud of the music we make — we love it — and we're fearless. If anyone puts us down, we don't care. If a kid picks up drumsticks because of our band, job done. Just to have guitars on the radio again is nice.'

Ash

America has often proved a musical bridge too far for overseas acts, but with it being the birthplace of rock'n'roll, guitar bands never go out of vogue. Luke and Michael can play guitar 'just like ringing a bell' (to quote Chuck Berry's all-American anthem, 'Johnny B. Goode'). With their infectious riffs and appropriately sun-kissed band name, 5SOS hoped to be in with a shout of winning over the 20,000 fans who'd crowded into the BB&T Center in Sunshine, Florida, on 13 June 2013 to see the opening show of the tour.

Fortunately, the extreme nerves that hampered their UK debut had long since evaporated and they effortlessly hit their stride, opening with 'Lost Boy'. They built up the momentum with 'Good Girls,' before easing back on the throttle with 'Heartbreak Girl' and 'Over and Over', before cranking it back up again with their own rendition of Katy Perry's 'Teenage Dream' and 'Out of My Limit', the video of which would receive its millionth hit while they were out on tour. They brought their seven-song set to a tumultuous finale with 'Try Hard' and had it not been for the unwritten rule that support acts aren't allowed an encore, they would

Wish you were here: backstage at the Billboard Music Awards, Las Vegas, May 2014.

surely have been welcomed back onto the stage. As was their nightly custom, the boys took to Facebook to thank everyone for what had been a truly 'AMAZING' experience.

The boys enjoyed similar amazing experiences in Miami, Louisville, and Columbus, and when the Take Me Home tour bus rolled into Nashville on 19 June, they got a taste of what life was like for the headliners. While out on a shopping trip, they were mobbed by fans.

With this being 1D's second world tour in as many years, Louis, Liam, Niall, Zayn and Harry had a catalogue of racy anecdotes about the lengths some overzealous fans would go to in the pursuit of their idols. The 5SOS boys had yet to experience returning to their hotel room after a show to find a fan hiding in the shower, but Mikey for one, is not fazed by the prospect. 'I reckon that could be funny, actually,' he told reporters.

The boys appeared far more interested in seeing America's landmarks. To the delight of their fans, many handsome new selfies began appearing on 5SOS's Tumblr pages, showing the boys outside the Johnson Space Center, New York's Empire State Building, the Washington Monument and more.

At the start of the tour the boys had let it be known they were keen to do some acoustic shows in-between the Take Me Home dates. The first of these was booked for 30 June at the Studio at Webster Hall in New York's trendy Greenwich Village. Only 300 tickets were available for this intimate gig and they sold out within a matter of hours. Fortunately for those 5SOSers who missed out, further acoustic shows were booked

> 'We listen to what the fans want and listen to what they want us to do.'
>
> Luke

in Boston, Chicago and Toronto. To further boost their profile stateside, the boys scheduled interviews with a string of local radio stations. Fans were also invited to meet-and-greet events on the days of the shows. One Direction may have been the main draw, but 5SOS were determined to leave their mark.

5 Seconds of Summer's involvement with the tour climaxed in four consecutive shows at the 20,000-capacity Staples Center in Downtown Los Angeles between 7 and 10 August. The boys had chopped and changed their set-list throughout the tour and for the final Staples show on 10 August they opened with 'Out of My Limit', but the expertise with which they worked the crowd left no one in any doubt that they were well within their comfort zone.

There was still the matter of twenty-five Australasian shows, but after taking their final LA bow the boys took to Facebook to thank 'the 1D boys' for giving them a 'special, amazing and crazy chance to show the world what we can do.'

★★★★

A further tie with One Direction came when 5 Seconds of Summer signed with Modest Management, the company who've been overseeing 1D's business affairs since they first got together on the 2010 series of *The X Factor*. Aside from 1D, Modest, (set up in 2003 by one-time president of BMG, Richard Griffiths and his partner Harry Magee), also have Little Mix, Olly Murs and Cheryl Cole on their books.

The boys viewed their signing with Modest as the next logical step in their career. Adam

5SOS perform at HMV's flagship store in Oxford Street, London, July 2014.

Wilkinson and Matt Emsell would continue seeing to their everyday needs, while Modest would represent them on the international stage. The boys saw it as a win-win situation, but the announcement didn't go down well with some fans owing to the adverse press Modest has gained for supposedly being controlling and unsympathetic to the needs of its artists. That the adverse press was largely coming from acts that had been dropped from Modest's books failed to assuage the fans' concerns.

With the online dissent showing no sign of abating, Luke responded to say the band were taking the fans' grievances seriously. 'We listen to what the fans want, and listen to what they want us to do,' he wrote. 'Then [we] respond to that and try and work with that. We try to make everybody happy.'

Meanwhile, several record companies had also expressed an interest in signing the boys, all of whom were eager to enter into negotiations with Modest Management. In view of 5SOS's feelings on this subject – Luke, Michael, Cal and Ash were determined to hold out for a label that would allow them artistic freedom – Richard Griffiths of Modest believed he'd found the perfect solution . . . with this in mind, he invited the CEO of Capitol Records, Steve Barnett, to accompany him to one of the One Direction/5 Seconds of Summer dates at Dublin's O2 Arena in March 2013.

Sixty-one-year-old Barnett had forged a reputation for allowing his acts absolute artistic freedom. While serving as CEO at Columbia Records, he'd presided over several highly successful stateside launch campaigns – including One Direction – and had also played a pivotal role in the band's subsequent American success.

It didn't take him long to recognise 5 Seconds of Summer's potential. 'They were infectious from the minute they walked onstage,' he told *Billboard* magazine. 'One and a half minutes into their first song, we said to Richard, "We are in!"'

A meeting was quickly set up and on seeing Steve Barnett shared their vision, 5SOS became Capitol Records' latest acquisition.

The boys were delighted with the deal they'd struck with Capitol as it not only allowed them the final say on every creative matter, but Barnett was happy for them to set up their own independent label that would operate under the Capitol umbrella.

As always, they involved their ever-expanding '5SOSFAM' in the decision-making in their new musical venture and posted the following message via Facebook:

HI. So we have some reallyyy exciting news for you ☺ After signing with Capitol Records last year, we've been talking about creating our own record label to release our music in partnership with them.

One of the reasons we've got to where we are is because we've always worked directly with you amazing people! What you already do to help us is incredible & having this label helps make sure that we can keep working directly with you guys as we (finally lol) release our first album.

Once the label's ready to launch, we'll give you more info on how you can be involved!!

First task – WE NEED A NAME!

We've come up with a couple below and need your help on choosing which one we go with ☺ Go on twitter and tweet us what you think using the below hashtags so we can pick our favourite. We know you're all just as weird as us so it can be as funny or serious as you like lolol

THANKS GUYS. X

#HIORHEYRECORDS
#TRYHARDRECORDS
#SOFTPUNKRECORDS
#BANANASMOOTHIERECORDS
#KETCHUPRECORDS

Of these five alternatives, Hi Or Hey was the clear fan-favourite. Once again, 5SOS opted to reveal the results – and the name of their newly incorporated label – via Facebook:

We have created this label for you guys. We have achieved so much together over the last two years and if it were not for you, we don't know where we would be.

As we get ready to release our debut album, we want to make sure that nothing changes and we keep working together to make all of our dreams become a reality.

We hear amazing stories from our fans every day of how you spread the 5SOS word. From our friends in the Philippines who have campaigned to get our songs on the radio for the last twelve months, to the amazing girls in France who postered all around Paris, we are blown away by your support. We love watching you all come together around the world for your 5SOS meet-ups.

'Hi Or Hey Records' means we can stay in control of our career. Things have gone pretty well with you and us the show so we want to keep it that way. We are building a website for the label where you will get to have your say in everything we are up to as well as show us all the incredible things you have been doing to spread the 5SOS word.

Life out loud: 5SOS bring a touch of pop punk to SiriusXM Studios, 22 July 2014.

Fresh from inking their lucrative deal with Capitol, the boys played two sell-out shows at KOKO in Camden Town on 26 and 27 November 2013. Growing up in their native Sydney, Luke, Mikey, Cal and Ash would likely have dreamed about playing such a venue. Back when it was known as the Music Machine, this grand old theatre turned live-music venue played host to a string of 5SOS's rock'n'roll heroes such as the Clash, the Ramones, and Iron Maiden.

KOKO boasts a 1,400 capacity, but with the boys having reportedly built up an eye-popping 300,000 followers on Twitter – not to mention having netted their 500,000th YouTube subscriber two days before the show – 5SOS were officially the hottest ticket in town that night. Indeed, such was the excitement that many of the teens and tweens lucky enough to be clutching a ticket were queuing up outside the venue hours before the doors opened, so as to be in with a chance of snagging a spot near the front of the stage.

★ ★ ★ ★

Hi Or Hey Records might mean Luke, Michael, Calum, and Ash could stay in control of their career, but Capitol was still calling the shots to a certain degree. Instead of returning home to Australia once their stateside touring commitments were done, it was agreed that the boys should remain in LA to write songs for their debut album.

Since Calum's first tentative attempt at setting lyrics to music – with the heartrendingly simple 'Gotta Get Out' – 5SOS could hardly wait to showcase their more mature new style. As Cal told the HMV website excitedly, 'When we started work on the album we got put in sessions with some really big writers. Before that we'd only really written in our bedrooms and so our songwriting has really moved on in that time.'

During an interview with *Coup de Main* magazine backstage at the Sheffield Leadmill, Luke explained the band's collaborative process in a little more detail. 'We usually go to write with other people and we'll go in groups of two,' he revealed. 'For instance, me and Michael will go to a songwriting session, and then Calum and Ashton will go to one. We usually come with an idea to write about, or the people that we're writing with will have an idea, and then we'll try and build a song around that.'

God save the SOS: a souvenir of Cal, Mike, Luke and Ash's visit to SiriusXM HQ, July 2014.

Michael's preferred method when trying to come up with a new song is to always write what's in his heart – whether others appreciate it or not. 'I think sometimes when you are writing, you try not to go too deep,' he told thoughtcatalogue.com. 'Sometimes the things you want to write about are not the type of things people want to hear. I think you have to put your soul into your music, and just write about whatever you feel like writing about . . . expressing your emotions in an honest way is always the best but sometimes it's hard to put some things in your music – you know? Knowing it will be released to masses of people, you get unsure.'

Even under pressure – with the deadline for the album looming large – 5SOS have never been the sort of band to waste time on petty squabbling. 'We are all on the same wavelength and are always going towards the same direction,' Michael revealed. 'We are always bouncing around a bunch of different ideas; we know what sounds best. We trust each other and just go with it. If you hear a part that kind of sucks, you just change it.'

Still buzzing from his time with Steve Robson (whose close connection with Busted was enough to leave Mike star-struck) the previous winter, the LA sessions saw Michael meet with another of his heroes: Alex Gaskarth from All Time Low. 'I think the day we collaborated with Alex was probably one of the best days of my life,' he gushed to *Coup de Main*. 'I still think about it. I still remember his face. He's such a beautiful man. He's one of my biggest idols and it was just so crazy. Now we're all friends with him and he's so supportive of us and it's just crazy. I never thought I'd be in this position.'

Luke was equally overcome when 5SOS collaborated with Benji and Joel Madden from Good Charlotte, the first band he ever saw live and the reason he started playing guitar. 'It's a standout for us because it was so incredible to write with the Madden brothers,' he told *60 Minutes* at the time of the album's release. 'They had this song they wrote a while ago ['Amnesia'], but couldn't find anyone it suited. The song has so much meaning. It's one of those songs that's really heartfelt on the album, and it's really special to us as a band.'

'We sort of met them through mutual friends and I guess we're really lucky,' Ash told pressparty.com about Benji and Joel. 'It's amazing to be able to work with them. We were looking for the right acoustic song to put on the album. We wanted something special and we heard that song for the first time . . . it was a big deal for us.'

What Michael and his starry-eyed bandmates were failing to grasp is that, for many of their high-profile collaborators, the appreciation was mutual. Speaking with *People* magazine

> 'I think you have to put your soul into your music and just write about whatever you feel like writing about.'
>
> Mike

in October 2014, Alex Gaskarth was incredibly complimentary about his time in the studio with gifted 'goofballs' Michael and Ash. 'They brought a ton of energy to the songs we wrote together,' he recalled. 'Calum and Luke were kind of the quiet ones at first. Once we got going, they started to come out of their shells.'

On being asked if he thought their sudden worldwide success might see the boys take their foot off the gas, he praised them all as 'such hard workers'. 'They're so dedicated to what they're doing that I don't see it slowing down for them.'

Overseeing the songwriting project was John Feldmann, the renowned American producer, songwriter and multi-instrumentalist. He was already known to the boys, having been introduced to them by a mutual friend during rehearsals for the Take Me Home tour the previous December.

'He's very smart,' Ash said of Feldmann. 'He knows how to keep his pop mentality. He doesn't try and cram in heavy breakdowns . . . he's very diverse.'

Reflecting on his time with 5SOS in an interview with *People* magazine, Feldmann had this to say of his pop-rock protégés: 'They're a real band. That was my first impression. They're all really good at what they do. I was just blown away.'

Feldmann's track-record speaks for itself. The co-writer and producer of countless bestselling albums and songs, Feldmann is perfectly placed to offer an opinion on whether or not fame has affected the boys. His verdict was as follows: 'They're still the same four boys. They're like brothers. They love each other and know where they came from.'

It wasn't all work and no play during their stay in LA, of course, and the boys made a video of themselves cruising around Hollywood in a Cadillac convertible sporting specially-hired comic-book superhero outfits: Luke and Ash brought a touch of Gotham City to the LA streets, posing as Batman and Robin; Michael was hidden beneath a snug-fitting Spiderman outfit, while Calum was a hunky, chunky Captain America.

During their sortie, the 'Awesome Foursome' called in at Capitol Records Tower and took their pillow pet mascot 'Ketchup' to a dog groomers before rounding their day off in an ice-cream parlour.

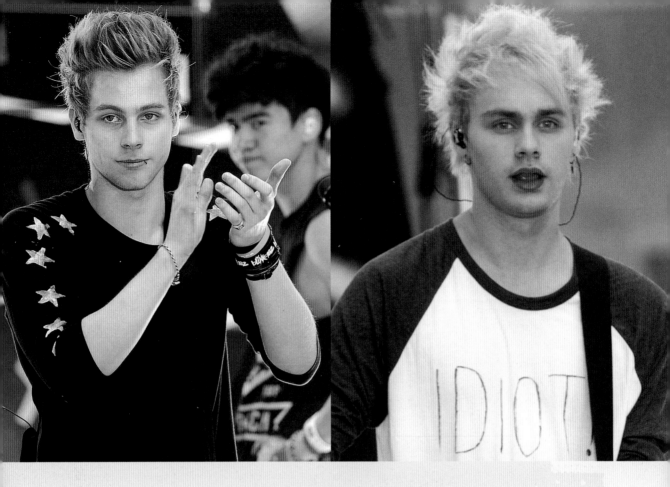

Chapter Six

One Hot Minute

'We wanted something to explain what the band
was all about. We get the boyband thing and we just
wanted to make a rocking pop song and say, "We're
5 Seconds of Summer and we're different". We haven't
released anything since we were about fifteen. The sort
of sound, the image and everything has changed.
We've grown up a little bit.'
Ash

On 21 March 2014, Capitol Records released 5 Seconds of Summer's first official worldwide single, 'She Looks So Perfect', on CD and digital download. The boys were understandably thrilled and took to their social media accounts to say they hoped the fans loved it, as well inviting everyone to 'GET NAKED' to mark the occasion.

'She Looks So Perfect' was one song to emerge from the LA writing sessions. The idea for the song started with Jake Sinclair, one of the seasoned songwriters brought onboard by John Feldmann. On a visit to his local American Apparel store, Sinclair espied a set of ads depicting girls wearing men's underpants and after noticing his girlfriend walking around in his t-shirt, Sinclair began scribbling down a set of sketchy lyrics. On his next meeting with 5SOS he mentioned the American Apparel ads. 'He showed us it and said, "This is what I've got, this is the idea,"' Ashton told Sugarscape.com. 'We thought it was really cute and sort of expanded on it.'

Ash may have thought the idea cute but his bandmate was far from convinced as the drummer later revealed to KIIS 106.5 Radio. 'Michael hated it,' he said. 'We wrote it in a day, and when we left the session, Michael said, "Man, that song sucked." So I was like, "Nah, man, it's a good song." So we pushed through and recorded it.'

Michael remembers it differently. In an interview with thoughtcatalog.com, he told how the summer anthem 'just kind of happened'.

From left to right: Luke, Mike, Cal and Ash stop traffic on the New York City streets, as part of the Today show, July 2014.

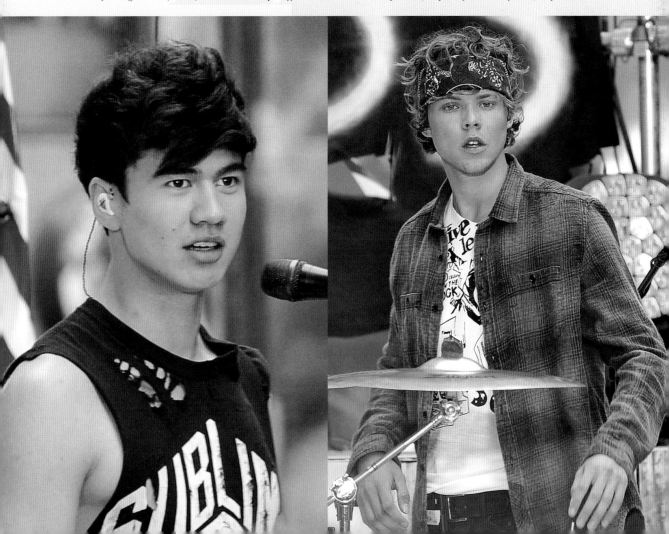

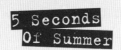

'We weren't expecting anything,' he added. 'We were just writing songs, it turned out to be what it was. We rolled with it. It just came out to be a really cool song in the end.'

Ash's determination to record the song would be rewarded ten-fold when the four-track *She Looks So Perfect* EP slammed onto the *Billboard* chart at number two, selling 143,000 copies in its first week of release.

The lyric video to 'She Looks So Perfect' had premiered on Vevo several weeks earlier and caused something of a stir as it featured a diverse range of everyday Americans going about their everyday lives . . . before suddenly losing it and stripping down to their American Apparel underwear in time with the beat.

'The director, Frank Borin, came to us with the idea and we're like, "That's absolutely perfect,"' Ash told *PopCrush*. 'He's like, "Yeah, the song puts people in a craze and makes them want to take their clothes off." And I was like, "Sounds good."'

> 'Frank came to us with this idea of the song just making people want to take their clothes off and we were like . . . that's amazing! And we like nudity, so we're in.'
>
> Luke

'I guess we were just looking around for ideas for the video stuff and Frank came to us with this idea of the song just making people want to take their clothes off or something?' Luke said in another interview. 'And we were like . . . That's amazing! And we like nudity, so we're in.'

The video received millions of hits within days of its Vevo premiere, yet given the millions American Apparel spends each year on advertising, one might have expected the clothing chain to be singing 5SOS's praises from the rooftops of its LA HQ following a reported ten percent surge in sales of their men's underwear range. Instead, there was nary a word.

With fans around the globe questioning the chain's ongoing silence on Facebook, Twitter and every other form of social media, the company – no doubt fearing the mighty 5SOSFam might choose to boycott their products – eventually capitulated and issued an official statement: 'We're flattered anytime we're mentioned in someone's music or art – especially a big summer anthem like this. Naturally, we also think women look great in our underwear.'

Although the EP had topped several charts around the world on pre-sales alone, the boys were still completely taken aback by its success. Ash was so overcome that he took to the band's Twitter account to personally thank their ten million followers. 'I actually cried of happiness today when I found out,' he gushed. 'I can't believe how we have all come together, you guys are the single reason this has happened, I love you all so much, we are so proud of you.'

★★★★

'She Looks So Perfect' wasn't due for release in the UK until the end of March 2014. Even so, the boys announced a seven-date tour of the country, culminating with a show at the Shepherd's Bush Empire in London on Monday, 3 March. Such was the demand for tickets, however, that an extra London show – again at the Shepherd's Bush Empire – was tagged onto the end. In each city of the tour, the boys called in at local radio stations, as well as staging meet-and-greets at various HMV stores up and down the country.

Rocking out with their socks out! 5SOS play the Today *show live in the heart of NYC, July 2014.*

Digital Spy had been monitoring the gathering fan-frenzy surrounding 5 Seconds of Summer from when the boys were out touring with One Direction the previous summer and sent one of its reporters along to the first of the Shepherd's Bush Empire shows to see if 5SOS had the talk to match the walk.

In what proved a 'let's-suck-it-and-see' critique, the review – which even made the mistake of referring to them as '5 Seconds *to* Summer' – archly referenced 'a Blink-182 riff here, a Green Day chant there, and a whole lot of All Time Low adoration everywhere,' before going on to suggest the boys were doing nothing more than taking 'inspiration from their punk-pop forefathers and [packaging] it into teen anthems'.

One questionable review from *Digital Spy*, however, did the *She Looks So Perfect* EP no harm whatsoever. In the UK, it went one better than it did stateside by topping the chart. The boys were holed up in a studio 'out in the middle of nowhere just outside Oxford' working on the hotly-anticipated *5 Seconds of Summer* album when they heard the news they were sitting pretty at the top of the UK chart.

Recalling the moment on *The Today Show*, Luke said: 'I remember running into Ashton's room and I was like, "We're number one!"'

The excitement spilled over onto their Facebook page: 'OFFICIAL NUMBER 1 IN THE UK. OMG OMG OMG we did it guys. Thanks to every single one of you and you know exactly what for. You mean everything to us really. We love all of you lots and lots and lots.'

There was precious little time to kickback and celebrate the achievement, however. If anything, the news had Capitol cracking the whip even harder to get the album ready, as Michael revealed in an interview with HMV: 'We were told that time [was] so short that we had to cram in recording six songs into two days – two long days.'

Breaking records (and hearts): 5SOS attend a signing session for 'She Looks So Perfect', Manchester HMV, March 2014.

'The FIFA time fell dramatically,' quipped Cal by way of corroborating Mikey's story.

Speaking with *Alter the Press* around the same time, the bassist revealed that they were pretty much finished with the debut album. 'We've written over a hundred songs now and we've finally whittled it down to twenty or twenty-five,' he said. 'We're really proud of it because we've been writing for so long . . . it's good to finally have a body of work of ours.'

He also confided that while *She Looks So Perfect* was a 'sample product of what the album's gonna be like', the full-length album would 'be a bit more diverse and a bit more colourful' – maybe owing to the eclectic range of co-writers who'd 'helped us a lot with our sound'.

No sooner were the finished tracks in the can than the boys headed over to Europe for their 5 Countries 5 Days tour, taking in Sweden, Germany, France, Italy and Spain. Prior to flying out to Stockholm for the opening show of 5 Countries 5 Days, the boys delivered another bombshell by announcing they would be serving as main support on the UK, European and North American legs of One Direction's Where We Are world tour. The opening show of the European leg would be at Dublin's Croke Park on 23 May 2014.

However, before hitting the road with their 1D buddies, the boys had their own US headline tour to think about. The Stars, Stripes and Maple Syrup tour was set to kick off with a show at the Fillmore in San Francisco on 11 April, and would take in shows in several cities the boys had previously visited on the Take Me Home Tour such as Los Angeles, Dallas, and Toronto – albeit in smaller venues – before culminating with a sell-out show at the 5,000-capacity Toyota Oakdale Theatre in Wallingford, Connecticut; their biggest headline show to date.

Once again, the media leapt upon the One Direction connection, but the boys refused to take the bait. 'The next One D is kind of an awkward comparison,' Ash told MTV UK in the wake of the announcement. 'They're amazing at what they do and we sort of do our own thing, and that's actually why we chose to go on the tour because it's so dynamic.'

As a parting gift for their UK fans, the boys announced on Facebook they'd 'made a bunch of "She Looks So Perfect" cassette tapes' for the seventh annual Record Store Day UK on Saturday, 19 April.

The freebie cassettes featured a special acoustic version of 'She Looks So Perfect,' and standard versions of 'Wherever You Are' and 'What I Like About You', as well as 'a song called "Pizza" [that] none of you have ever heard before'.

Calum would later dismiss 'Pizza' as nothing more than 'a joke . . . something we just mucked around with,' in conversation with *Alter the Press*. They'd seen the tape as a chance for them to involve the 5SOSers of the UK in something 'cool' – but that was all. 'They had to go find it in record

> 'As a band, we really like setting challenges and stuff for the fans. It's kind of old-school as well, so that's nice.'
> Calum

stores,' he said. 'As a band, we really like setting challenges and stuff for the fans. It's kind of old school as well, so that's nice.'

★★★★

The world was fast becoming 5SOS's oyster, but home is where the heart is and the boys had no intention of forgetting their fans in Oz. Following a five-day breather, they got the seven-date There's No Place Like Home tour underway with a sell-out show at Sydney's 1,600-capacity Enmore Theatre.

This was the boys' first hometown show since the One Direction Take Me Home tour the previous October and – in what was now becoming a familiar scene wherever they travelled in the world – the pavement outside the theatre was teeming with giddy girls, the majority of whom had been camped out since first light in the hope of catching a glimpse of the band arriving at the venue.

The boys' families also found themselves in the spotlight, with Calum's mum, Joy, coming in for particular attention as she took her seat. And those girls who'd yet to grab a selfie with their idols rushed over and besieged Luke's brothers, Ben and Jack, and Ash's kid brother, Harry.

This, of course, was nothing compared to the reaction when the boys – dressed in their by now customary stage threads of skinny jeans and black cut-off vintage rock band T-shirts – emerged from the wings. Aside from a crescendo of ear-piercing shrieks, the hall was suddenly awash with flashing lights from more than a thousand outstretched phone screens as the boys plug in and launch into the opening song, '18'.

After the show the boys would admit to being nervous at playing in front of their families, with Calum going so far as to tell the crowd that 'tonight we have to prove to our parents why it's worthwhile that we dropped out of school'.

Cal's tongue was obviously firmly in his cheek as he spoke this line, but the 5SOS parents gave their seal of approval just the same. And his dad was observed gleefully singing along to 'Heartache on the Big Screen' with obvious pride.

Chapter Seven

Six-String Superheroes

'We want to be a credible live band so people would come and see us and say, "That's better than we hear on the record". It's so fascinating that people say, "They can really play". We didn't know it was a weird thing that we could actually play instruments and write music.'

Luke

O n 16 June – with 5 Seconds of Summer out on the European leg of One Direction's Where We Are tour – Capitol decided to crank up the momentum for the release of their upcoming album (slated for later that month). They did so by issuing 'Don't Stop,' 5SOS's second international single. In the US, where the album wasn't set for release until 22 July, an alternate track, 'Good Girls,' was issued.

Steve Barnett and the other suits at Capitol were well aware that they had a hit act on their hands with 5SOS, but even they must have been taken aback by the online response to 'Don't Stop'. Within 48 hours of its premiere on Vevo, the promo video racked up two million views.

5SOS had already spent a considerable amount of time larking about in LA in their hired superhero outfits, but the 'Don't Stop' video saw them take their comic-book fantasy to the extreme, with each bandmate adopting his own persona: Luke morphed into 'Dr Fluke', Michael was 'Mike-Ro-Wave', Cal became 'Cal-Pal', while Ash was 'Smash'. Viewing the 'making of' video, it's obvious the boys enjoyed themselves immensely. Ash declared being a superhero 'pretty awesome' and relished the chance to run around in tight underwear. Michael, however, thought it only fair to warn the 5SOSFam of the obvious downside to being

Penmanship: 5SOS return to Manchester HMV to sign copies of their self-titled debut album, 30 June 2014.

a comic-book crime-fighter. 'I would've spent every day in those suits,' he said, 'except when you need to pee . . . that's really hard.'

The boys were desperate for 'Don't Stop' to emulate the success of 'She Looks So Perfect' in giving them a second UK number one. Luke, especially, was waiting on tenterhooks to hear how the release would perform. 'I hope for another number one, but we don't want to get too excited,' he told the *Daily Mail*. 'Number one never gets boring; it's such a big thing. I don't know what I would do if it happened again.'

To help spread the word about the upcoming release, the boys staged a series of in-store signings at several HMVs up and down the country, where an extra 1,000 copies of the single were made available close to the chart cut-off date. Despite their best efforts, however, they were to be denied the top spot by former X *Factor* finalist, Ella Henderson.

They would also have to settle for second spot on the UK album chart, losing out to ginger wunderkind, Ed Sheeran. Over in the States, however, it was a different story. *5 Seconds of*

> 'Number one never gets boring; it's such a big thing.
> I don't know what I would do if it happened again.'
>
> Luke

Summer debuted at number one on the *Billboard* Hot 100, selling an astonishing 259,000 copies. Not only was it the biggest first-week sales for a debut album by any group in eight years, but it also gave them the honour of being the first Australian act to have their debut album take the number one spot in America. Not even hard-rock heroes AC/DC managed this feat.

The European leg of 1D's Where We Are tour wound up with a show at the Estadio Vicente Calderón in Madrid on 11 July. After this, 5SOS jetted back to the UK to play Hallam FM's Summer Live event – a huge gig staged at Sheffield's Motorpoint Arena on 18 July. They were due to hook up with One Direction again in Toronto on 1 August for the opening date on the tour's North American leg, but they chose to reintroduce themselves to America a tad earlier by jetting into New York to appear on *Today*, the fifth longest-running show on US television, on 22 July.

Aside from performing 'Amnesia' and 'She Looks So Perfect' live in the *Today* studio, the boys would be staging a mini-gig in Rockefeller Plaza to celebrate the album's US release. America's tween queens had been falling in love with 5 Seconds of Summer since their stateside appearances on the Take Me Home tour the previous June. Yet the fan-frenzy they'd witnessed on their more recent headlining Stars, Stripes and Maple Syrup tour was nothing compared to the scenes that greeted the boys' arrival in Manhattan.

They literally brought central New York to a standstill, drawing an even bigger crowd than the estimated 15,000 that gathered for One Direction when they appeared on the show to promote *Take Me Home* in November 2012. According to the show's producers, fans had been camping out in Rockefeller Plaza and the surrounding streets for several days to ensure they bagged the best vantage points.

'Seriously, this is the most incredible thing that's probably ever happened to us,' Ash told *Today*'s hosts. 'Right now, it's amazing. It's definitely not another day at the office.'

We will rock you: bringing a touch of attitude to Capital's Summertime Ball, Wembley Stadium, June 2014.

It was a similar scene in downtown LA two days later when the ultra-busy Hawthorne Street was closed off to traffic while the boys performed a four-song set on the *Jimmy Kimmel Live* block party.

★★★★

The boys' collaborations with the likes of Steve Robson, Alex Gaskarth, Joel and Benji Madden, and Jake Sinclair, had obviously flavoured their writing style, yet the songs on the album were nonetheless highly personal to the 5SOS boys themselves. More importantly, they also reflected the life experiences of the 5SOSFam – many of whom were living through exactly the same angst-ridden teen issues as Luke, Ash, Cal and Mike – enabling the boys to connect with their audience like never before.

'I think that a lot of the songs are quite deep at times, we've been through a lot of stuff,' Ash explained to musictakeabow.com. 'A lot has happened to us in the past few years. We've been lonely; we've been happy; we've been sad. If you really listen closely to the EP and the album that's coming out, it's real stuff that's sort of happened to us.'

When reviewing the album, *Sugarscape* mentioned the boys having teamed up with some massive names, before playfully adding that the twelve 'anthems of youth; acne, mood-swings and all that other fun teenage bullsh*t' were still the work of 'those four derpfaced fellas from high school'.

Rolling Stone observed that, regardless of the decade, teenagers never seemed to tire of 'cute boys singing about babes and clothes,' before praising the single – and the album's opening

NRJ to burn: 5SOS strike a pose outside the Parisian radio station, NRJ, April 2014.

track – 'She Looks So Perfect', as a 'sublime three-minute wallop of "hey-ey-ey-ey"s, crunchy chords and gym-class angst'.

Billboard magazine's Jason Lipshutz astutely opined that, at this point in their career, 5 Seconds of Summer were a 'hybrid of two musical ideas: a pop-punk act where the "pop" greatly [outweighed] the "punk", and [that] the guitar riffs were plentiful but [didn't] cut hard enough to have parents concerned'. He also praised the boys' 'pretty ingenious aesthetic' in inviting fans of both genres to 'come together, sing along to the pristine choruses and head-bang ever so slightly', before declaring *5 Seconds of Summer* 'a delightful debut from a group that cannot be easily pigeonholed, and is worth paying attention to'.

The *New York Daily News* was particularly enthusiastic about 'She Looks So Perfect,' ranking the song as its 'favourite trash single of the summer . . . an insanely tasty piece of candy-pop with a lyric that's both witty and saucy,' while HMV.com hailed it as 'stomping, full-blooded pop-rocker with a colossal chorus'. Indeed, there's a good reason why 5SOS chose this track as the album opener. In the eyes of Ash – and the rest of the band – 'She Looks So Perfect' was 'the perfect song to really represent us'.

'Don't Stop,' which Luke says is about 'the girl that everyone wants to take home from the party,' was also singled out as being another perfect pop song to 'get you up on your feet [or] head-bang in your car'.

'Good Girls' was another product of the London song-writing sessions of December 2102, with several writers receiving co-credits along with Ash and Michael. Scouting for Girls' Roy Stride and Stride's occasional writing partner, Josh Wilkinson were two other contributors. Andpop.com described the track as sounding like a 'throwback to a nineties pop hit that would be featured in a romantic comedy,' owing to it being 'young and fun' with 'just the right amount of cheekiness'. The reviewer could well imagine the song's sassy chorus – 'good girls are bad girls that haven't been caught' – emblazoned on T-shirts everywhere. According to Calum, this famously cheeky line came from Stride. Though he initially presented it to Cal and Luke, both boys instantly recognised it as being more suited to Ash and Michael's lyrical style and passed it to them.

'Kiss Me Kiss Me,' the first of the trio of Alex Gaskarth collaborations that appear on the album's standard twelve-track listing, encapsulates the bittersweet sensations the boys were experiencing while out on tour. 'It's about meeting someone you really liked spending time with and not knowing if you can let it go,' Luke explained.

'You only get so much time with the friends that you make,' Ash added. 'You move and you move and you move . . . this song is about making the most of the time you have with people you meet on the road.'

> 'This album is going to have a twist of punk and gospel to take a new spin on pop culture.'
> Luke

'18' continues the fun, up-beat vibe that flows throughout the album. The opening couplet suggests the song is another ode to the frustrations of waiting for adulthood, but it's actually about a boy's obsession with an older woman.

Alter the Press declared 'Everything I Didn't Say' as the 'power anthem that every album needs,' while complimenting its 'taking a slightly different path' after the full-throttle opening salvo of the first five tracks. Calum and Ash wrote the song with John Feldmann and Nicholas 'RAS' Furlong, another of the established songwriter-producers Feldmann regularly called upon.

Speaking about the concept behind the song on YouTube – in a video that analyses the album track-by-track – Ash explained: '[It's about] when you're in a relationship and then you break up, and you're like, "Man, I didn't really commit to that" . . . the other person put a lot more effort in than you did and you regret it.'

In the same video Michael admitted that, of all the songs within the 5SOS canon, 'Everything I Didn't Say' was 'the one song I wish I'd written'.

'Beside You' is another slow-tempo, heartfelt offering, which *Billboard* complimented for its 'more successful pairing of Luke's yearning vocals with the soaring melody'.

'End up Here' – the second track to credit Alex Gaskarth as a co-writer – marks another change in tempo, kicking the album back into gear with crashing guitars and catchy hand-clap choruses, driven along on a keyboard-synthesiser hook. 'We needed a song that lifts the crowd . . . a party song,' Ash said of the track. 'We wanted to write something up-tempo that gets the crowd jumping.'

With its lilting piano chord intro, 'Long Way Home' showcases Gaskarth's softer side. The song resulted from Ash and Michael's first session with their idol. 'All Time Low are basically the reason I started playing guitar and singing,' Michael gushed in an interview with *PopCrush*. 'So to get the opportunity to write with him, it's just insane.'

'He definitely got us,' Ash said of the collaboration. 'Within fifteen minutes of getting there [in the studio], we had this chorus idea.'

'Heartbreak Girl' – another song to be carried over from the London sessions – quickly found its way into the hearts of 5SOSers everywhere. In fact, this track premiered as a free

download in early 2013. It was also the first 5SOS video to top one million views on YouTube. 'It's good to see the crowd singing every single word of this song,' Ash enthused. 'It's cool 'cause it means a lot to us as it [represents] the first steps we took with coming over to the UK.'

Billboard's Jason Lipshutz singled out 'Amnesia' as the song which 'established itself as 5 Seconds of Summer's successful Serious Pose,' while demonstrating the boys' 'versatility'. What he failed to understand, however, was why the boys had 'buried' this stand-out track at the end of the album. 5SOS themselves, however, definitely don't see the song as 'buried'. Written by Benji and Joel Madden of Good Charlotte, Michael sees it as a beautiful end to the album. 'They wrote it a while ago and couldn't find anyone it suited,' he explained. 'They were saving it for the "special people". It's really heartfelt [and] special to us as a band.'

★★★★

The media has long blamed *The X Factor* and other TV talent shows for the paucity of up-and-coming teen bands, few of whom seem able to play their own instruments or write their own songs. 5SOS were adept at both. Yet, unbelievably, these same journalists seemed more intent on finding fault with their style than praising their creative efforts.

While it's true that only sticks and stones can break bones, name-calling can bruise the hardiest of egos. And one barb in particular that would have stung the boys came from *Kerrang!* editor, James McMahon. The magazine was in the process of compiling a Green Day tribute CD to commemorate the tenth anniversary of the band's now-iconic album *American Idiot* for its forthcoming July issue. McMahon, after listening to 5SOS's version of the title track, went online to publicly dismiss the band as 'rubbish'. The boys may have been choked, but their fans had plenty to say in their defence and unleashed a torrent of online abuse at both McMahon and *Kerrang!* demanding that he retract his comments.

> 'It's nice to see people realise we're trying to do something different. It's really cool.'
>
> Ash

Perhaps realising the detrimental effect the backlash could have on sales, McMahon went on the damage-limitation defensive. 'I did a tweet saying that 5 Seconds of Summer are rubbish,' he said. 'Because, y'know, I'm a 33-year-old man with a beard. Now I am feeling THE WRATH. Here's what I think about 5SOS as *Kerrang!* editor. They are rubbish but if they help somebody get into the Descendants one day, then AWESOME.'

Kerrang!'s 'love/hate' relationship with 5 Seconds of Summer went into distortion overdrive when the boys were voted Best International Newcomer at the magazine's 2014 awards ceremony, held at the Troxy Theatre in Stepney, East London on 12 June. When posting the nominees in each category on its website earlier in the month, the magazine proudly declared that its readership had 'voted in your thousands', yet when 5SOS's name was read out – according to the *Guardian* – it was greeted by a chorus of boos.

This was churlish in the extreme for, while the other nominees in this category – Crossfaith, Issues, State Champs and We Came as Romans – were all promising new acts, none could match 5SOS's astounding achievement to date.

Keeping it low-key: Ash, Cal, Mike and Luke make a relaxed appearance at Manchester's Key 103 Live, July 2014.

On being asked for his thoughts on 5SOS winning the award, rather than risk entering in a war of words with McMahon, Luke simply stated how much it meant to the band, as they'd all avidly read *Kerrang!* from cover to cover whilst growing up in Sydney.

Despite the massive exposure 5SOS enjoyed on the back of scoring a US number-one album, their association with One Direction meant some people still saw them as 1D take-two. Fortunately for 5SOS, not every listener subscribes to this same narrow-minded point of view. 'Someone said to me the other day when they came to see our show, they were like, it's amazing to see people going crazy for some people with guitars on stage,' Ash said on the US TV show, *Extra.* 'They said they hadn't seen that in about ten years. It's nice to see people realise we're trying to do something different. It's really cool.'

Ash expanded on this when he and Luke appeared on the Fernando and Greg talk show on 99.7 NOW. 'When people say, "Oh, you boys play your instruments," they go, "That's really weird". It's weird to us because we thought that's just what you do. People listen to our songs and say, "Did you play on this?" What do you mean? Yeah, it's our song.

'It's really nice that some young people are getting pumped over some boys with guitars – that is really cool,' he continued. 'It's not a struggle to be taken seriously. I think if you listen to our music and stuff and give us ten minutes to – I don't know – understand the band. It is really not a struggle to be taken seriously it is just a struggle to dodge people's instant thoughts on the band . . . people go, "These boys have girls outside their hotel it must be a boyband. How good are their dance moves?" And we don't blame them because the type of band we are doesn't exist at the moment except for us.'

Chapter Eight

Rocking Out With Their Socks Out

'We are still surprised that girls like our band . . .
if you weren't a footballer then you weren't attractive.
But it's cool that girls like our band. We're very lucky
people want photos with us because one day they won't.'

Ash

In July 2014, the boys unveiled dates for their own headlining world tour. To the excitement of the 5SOSFam, the boys' Rock Out With Your Socks Out tour would take in more than 60 shows across the UK, Europe, Australasia and North America – with every chance of extra dates being added due to unprecedented demand. Opening date was set for 4 May 2015 at the MEO Arena in Lisbon, Portugal. The tour would close in spectacular style at the Cruzan Amphitheatre in West Palm Beach, California, on 13 September.

Shortly after the announcement, Calum gave *Alter the Press* a tantalising insight to what fans could expect from 5SOS's first ever headlining world tour. 'The album has got a lot of songs that are high-energy that you can rock out to, and I want to get that energy and throw it out to the audience in a live experience,' he said. 'I want them to leave feeling like they ran a marathon basically! I want it to be loud and rock and high-energy. I want it to be fun and capture the humour of the band at the same time. It'll be all those things mashed into one.

'The core thing for us is lighting,' he went on. 'We don't do too much with the stage; we just do things that emphasise our stage craft. We're a guitar band, so we don't have things that will propel us into the air! It's just a stage that you can rock out on.'

The boys had enjoyed worldwide exposure on two One Direction tours. Now they were in a position to go out under their own steam, *Alter the Press* was curious to know who would be 5SOS's support act of choice. 'We see bands everyday whether they're local or well-known bands and we always say, "Man, they could come out on tour with us!" but nothing is confirmed,'

Left: 5SOS proudly flaunt their Moon Man trophy at the 2014 VMAs. Below: onstage at the iTunes Festival, held at Camden's historic Roundhouse, September 2014.

Calum said. 'We always see bands that could add a core dynamic to our own. It's kind of hard right now. We speak about it a lot.'

Touring the world, riding shotgun with 1D, had been a learning curve for the boys and Luke had paid particular attention in class. 'I've learned how to make 10,000 or even 70,000 people feel that they're part of it,' he told the *New York Times*. 'It's not just playing the songs and playing them perfectly. You've got to be this massive entity on stage and just bring people in and make them have a good time.'

> '**We're a guitar band,
> so we don't have things that
> will propel us into the air.
> It's just a stage that you
> can rock out on.**'
>
> **Calum**

'It's incredible to even have the opportunity to create an amphitheatre/arena show,' Ash said in another interview. 'I'm really looking forward to that. I really want people just to leave the show going, "Wow, I can't wait to see a 5 Seconds of Summer show again." I'd like to be known for our live shows, so I really want to put on an experience for our fans.'

The US leg of the tour wasn't set to get underway until 17 July 2015 at the Mandalay Bay Event Centre in Las Vegas, but their American fans – or at least those living on the West Coast – wouldn't have to wait for then as the boys announced a one-off show at the LA Forum on Saturday, 15 November 2014. Tickets for the Forum show went on sale on Saturday, 26 July, with a tantalising promise: the first five hundred people in line would be invited to a special meet-and-greet with the boys. Of course, starry-eyed 5SOSers began queuing up the evening before.

The day itself was full of surprises as those queuing for tickets enjoyed a live Mariachi band covering 5SOS songs. There was also a stash of promotional giveaways, but the best treat came once all the tickets had been snapped up; at this point, the boys emerged to do an impromptu three-song acoustic set: 'She Looks So Perfect,' 'Beside You' and 'Amnesia'.

What didn't come as much of a surprise to anyone, of course, was the news that a second Forum show had been booked for Sunday, 16 November, to cope with the phenomenal demand for tickets. A third US show was also added for Thursday, 13 November at the Ak-Chin Pavilion in Phoenix, Arizona. Although making their way to the Forum was at the forefront of the boys' thinking, playing the Ak-Chin Pavilion would still be pretty awesome – if only because it was where Green Day had recorded 'Cigarettes And Valentines' for their 2011 live album, *Awesome as F****.

To coincide with the Forum date the boys took to Twitter to announce the first-ever 'Derp Con' fan event on the afternoon of the second show:

Derp Con 2014 is us bringing people from all over the world to the USA to fight ninjas, internet haters and join in some serious banding. We are launching a worldwide competition where entrants (i.e. you!) have the chance to be a part of this between November 15/16. As part of your reward, you will fly over to Los Angeles with a friend (prize incl. flights & accom) to attend Derp Con and come hang out at the Forum for our biggest headline show yet! There we will draw our battle lines and prepare to fight our foes. None shall stand in our way.

Derping seems to have become synonymous with 5 Seconds of Summer. According to the *Urban Dictionary*, 'derping' or 'herping the derp' is traditional gaming jargon for 'engaging in a

Tongues out! Backstage at the iHeartRadio Festival, September 2014.

discussion without any serious intent'. Another description of derping is to be 'messing about: i.e. "Why didn't you respond to my text?" "Oh, sorry, I was too busy derping around."'

Fans can now buy official 5SOS T-shirts bearing the slogan: '5 Seconds of Summer – derping since 2011'. During a backstage Skype interview with *Coup de Main* magazine at the Sheffield Leadmill back in February, Mikey said that 'Derpy' was the name the boys had given to a My Little Pony toy that they'd adopted as the band's mascot.

Unless there were any last-minute additions to the 5SOS tour schedule, the boys were set to wind down 2014 with several festive flings commencing with the 99.7 Triple Ho in San Jose, on 3 December, and ending twelve days later at Hot 99.5's Jingle Ball in Washington DC at the Verizon Centre as part of a star-studded line-up including Ariana Grande, Calvin Harris, Demi Lovato, OneRepublic, Iggy Azalea, Jessie J and Rita Ora.

★★★★

In the fifteen years since their inception, the Teen Choice Awards have become recognised by discerning teenagers across the globe as the litmus test to what's hot and what's not. Although 5SOS narrowly lost out to their pals One Direction in the Best Group and Best Break-Up Song categories, they were voted Choice Music: Breakout Group, as well as the Choice Summer Music Star: Group.

The ceremony was staged at the Shrine Auditorium in Los Angeles. Owing to long-standing commitments the boys couldn't attend in person. Instead, they accepted their surfboard awards via a pre-recorded video in which they playfully appeared with bath towels wrapped about their waists.

The sight of the boys' tanned and perfectly toned torsos obviously wasn't enough for some

BRIT pack: 5SOS arrive at the 2014 BRIT Awards, held on 19 February at London's O2 Arena.

fans and within minutes of the video being aired, they took to social media to point out how Ash appeared to have an unusual bulge protruding from beneath his towel.

With interest in what might have been going on under his towel refusing to die down Ash joined in the fun. 'Apparently I had a boner in the acceptance video,' he joked via Twitter. 'I love you guys, thanks for everything you do for us, fighting for us, following us and supporting the music.'

The boys already had one MTV award sitting on the mantelpiece, and later in the month 'Buzzworthy's Fan-Favourite Breakthrough Band of 2013' flew out to Los Angeles to perform at the MTV Video Music Awards. Having wowed the crowd with 'Amnesia', they came away at the end of the evening with the Best Lyric Award for the video to 'Don't Stop'.

In late July, 5 Seconds of Summer were announced as part of the 2014 iTunes Festival line-up which was being staged at the Roundhouse in Camden Town. The festival was set to run for thirty nights through September, and although the line-up boasted some of the biggest names in rock and pop, there was only one date ringed on the calendar of any self-respecting 5SOSer – Thursday, 4 September. On this day, Ash, Luke, Mikey and Cal were scheduled to play. Unlike other festivals, however, tickets for the iTunes shows could not be purchased; they had to be won via the iTunes website or through various radio competitions.

Knowing their rock history as they do, the boys were thrilled to be invited as they'd be treading the same hallowed stage previously occupied by many of their all-time favourite bands, including the Rolling Stones, Led Zeppelin, Pink Floyd, the Clash and the Ramones. An added bonus came with news that another hero of theirs – former Busted frontman, Charlie Simpson – would be supporting them on the night.

Although Busted scooped two BRIT Awards, the more rock-orientated Simpson became disillusioned with penning and playing commercial pop music. In late 2003, he formed 'Fightstar' in secret with Alex Westaway, and would spend the next twelve months or so living a double life sneaking off to rehearse with Fightstar after completing his Busted obligations.

In scenes highly reminiscent of when the boys played their two sell-out shows a few hundred yards down the road at KOKO the previous November, hundreds of emotionally-charged teens gathered outside the Roundhouse, long before the opening of the doors. The glaring difference between those KOKO shows and tonight, however, is that a sizeable number of these girls also had their boyfriends in tow; many of whom either had their long fringes swept rakishly across their foreheads or were sporting bandanas in homage of their 5SOS idols.

'I think eventually we are going to evolve into being more accessible to dudes. As our fans grow up, so will our music,' Michael told thoughtcatalogue.com. 'I think it's just a matter of

'We like our shows to be a big party vibe, y'know?
We want it to be an amazing experience . . .
We want a show that fans can get involved in.'

Luke

time. We are definitely not going anymore pop than we are now. All bands can start being really cool at some point to boys, we can grow into it. Hopefully we will see more dudes at the shows.'

The Roundhouse has come to be regarded as something of a rock shrine, and there were those within the British media who were affronted at the thought of a 'boyband' playing here. But each and every one of the lucky ticket holders could have told them that 5 Seconds of Summer were worthy of the praise being lavished on them in teen mags around the globe.

Charlie Simpson was rightfully given a rousing welcome, and his 'acoustic rock' set was peppered throughout with polite chants of 'Charlie, Charlie, Charlie' . . . but this was nothing compared to the sonic tsunami that greeted the arrival of Luke, Mikey, Calum and Ash on the stage.

The *Sydney Morning Herald*'s senior music writer, Bernard Zuel, had been flown in courtesy of Apple to cover the event. Zuel may have raised a bemused eyebrow at the multicoloured hair and mix'n'match clothes of fans and band alike – especially Michael, whose vivid red shock of hair was reminiscent of a 'young Johnny Rotten' – but he came away at the end of the evening knowing he'd seen a 'perfectly accomplished pop-rock band who could play well, could work the room with energy and enthusiasm . . . and who have enough good songs to punctuate an hour, if not fill it [with] the fizziness of straight pop, the bounciness of pop rock and the moves and occasionally the aggression of straight rock'.

As if a headlining world tour wasn't enough, on 24 September, MTV US reported that the band was working on songs for their follow-up album. 5SOS had recently teased their fans by posting a picture of a sound desk on Instagram. 'Recording some NEW NEW stuff,' read the caption. Now it was official. '"Trying" is the key word,' Ash revealed. 'We've been trying to fit it in. We've been so busy lately. We've been on tour for a few months, so we've just been playing and doing lots of promo, but we are definitely feeling creative again and excited to write a second album.'

The boys still had a stock of unfinished songs left over from the London sessions, but opportunities to take a second look at these had been few and far between. 'I think when you're on the road you've got to just live out what's happening, then when you get back to the studio you've got a lot to write about,' Ash said. 'I don't want to write the same album again, so I go out there and see what life has for me . . . then I'll go back and write about it. We've got a lot of time coming up, actually, to write and record again, so I'm really looking forward to that 'cause I'm feeling like I miss that at the moment.'

Calum also prefers to focus on other things than writing whilst out on the road. Like Ash, he is excited at the prospect of a new album. 'We learnt a lot from writing the first one and we're excited to continue evolving as a band, to have something a little bit older and mature,' he told *Alter the Press*. 'It's still very early, but we're sending around demos. That's about it at the moment. We're still focused on touring, so there's not too much writing going on right now.'

As for the musical direction of the new recording, Cal and the boys are undecided. 'We have so many ideas and I'm really ready to mature our sound – definitely a more organic sound, just drum and bass and two guitars,' he added. 'We'd like to write a lot of it ourselves this time but

'We don't know whether we are supposed to be keeping secrets or not . . . We want to have some surprises up our sleeves.'

Ash

work with the same people and maybe one or two new people. We heard from Simple Plan actually when we were in Canada. We would like to work with bands like that who are really cool. We've actually written a lot of songs that have never been released that aren't quite right for us. Some are too heavy, some are too soft and bands are like, "I'd really like to use this song!" And that's a cool thing to experience as well.'

Rumours that the boys would be releasing a fourth single from *5 Seconds of Summer* also began to circulate. When quizzed on this subject, Ash responded with a shrug. 'We don't know whether we're supposed to be keeping secrets or not. We want to have some surprises up our sleeves,' he replied mysteriously . . . and he was clearly hiding something, because on 10 October, 5SOS posted the video for 'Good Girls' on YouTube. The single is set for release on 17 November and is more or less guaranteed to be a hit, given that the video – in which 5SOS appear as a naughty schoolboy string quartet – has already racked up over seven million views.

Another story to surface in October was that of One Direction's secret investment in 5SOS. Louis supposedly discovered the Aussie band by chance whilst browsing YouTube, but – on a trawl through the files at Companies House in London – a reporter from *Billboard* magazine uncovered evidence to suggest otherwise. In fact One Direction are co-owners of a company entitled 5SOS LLP, which means Louis, Liam, Niall, Zayn and Harry stand to profit from the success of their Aussie tourmates. Whatever the truth about this business connection, however, the friendship between the two bands seems entirely genuine.

'Cause I'm just a teenage dirtbag, baby: the four goofballs of 5SOS. Clockwise from top-left: Luke, Mike, Ash and Cal.

And the winner is . . . 5SOS enjoy their moment in the limelight at the MTV Video Music Awards, August 2014.

5 October 2014 marked 5SOS's final show on the Where We Are tour. Even so, the boys' schedule remained as manic as ever. Upcoming events on the 5SOS calendar included the final of X *Factor Australia* (13 October), the BBC Radio One Teen Awards (Wembley, London; 19 October) *and* a jet-setting promotional visit to Japan. First up was the X *Factor* gig back in Sydney. As per usual, the boys were mobbed on arrival at Kingsford Smith Airport. Even after an eighteen-hour flight, Luke, Mike, Cal and Ash were more than happy to sign autographs and pose for selfies with the home-grown 5SOSers awaiting them there. If the boys were weary, they definitely didn't show it. As they took to the X *Factor* stage the following day, 5SOS were given a thunderous welcome – good for morale, but hard on Mikey's ears. On tour with 1D the previous month, the guitarist had consulted a doctor about his hearing. The specialist confirmed he'd lost the ability to hear 'high-pitched noises' in his right ear due to constant screaming at shows.

Over in London, UK 5SOSers waited eagerly for *their* chance to get up-close and personal with the guys. Alas, 5SOS never even boarded their plane out of Oz, as the day after X *Factor* Ash was rushed to hospital with terrible pains in his abdomen. A press release followed, confirming he'd had to have his appendix removed and was now recuperating. 'Gutted' to have to disappoint their fans, the boys took to the web to announce that, while Ash was on the mend, they were going to have to cancel their set at the Radio One Teen Awards. 'We are so sorry to everyone that had planned on seeing us. We were so excited to come see you all and we never want to make any of you sad . . . We hope you understand!'

The promo trip to Japan was also off the agenda. 'Sup guys,' Ash tweeted from his bed on 15 October. 'I'm so sorry to anyone I've let down, I promise we will make it up to ya! I'll be better soon, thanks for all the love xx' Meanwhile, Luke had his own special instructions for the 5SOSFam. 'Send @Ashton5SOS love and Vegemite,' he posted.

Ash promised to be 'back up and running in no time' – and this is exactly how it happened. On 17 October, he was discharged from hospital. Just ten days later, a swoon-inducing snap appeared on Twitter, showing the handsome drummer stripped to the waist for a surfing trip with Cal and three of their mates back home. Aussie sunshine is clearly the best medicine . . .

At the time of writing, the lads are most definitely 'back on the road (minus one band appendix)'. Fresh from a fun appearance on *The Ellen DeGeneres Show*, 5SOS are currently holed up in 'a little town called LA or somethin,' reported Ash over Twitter. 'Ellen is awesome,' he added. 'Thanks so much for letting us rock out – happy days!' Of course, he was referring to 5SOS's performance of 'Good Girls' live in the studio. But the fun-loving blonde TV host had something more than a conventional interview in store for the Aussie boys. In fact, she had a fake lift installed for the occasion – allowing groups of smitten 5SOSers a cheeky glimpse of Luke, Mikey, Cal and Ash, before the doors slid shut between them and their crushes. 'Awesomeness at the *Ellen* show,' is how Ash summed up the experience.

> 'Because we're such good friends we keep ourselves grounded. There's no diva behaviour . . . yet.'
>
> Michael

On 9 November, 5SOS were thrilled to win three gongs at the MTV Europe Music Awards. Though they weren't able to attend the glitzy Glaswegian ceremony in person, they thanked their fans via video link, as well as sending 'big love' online. 'You guys are incredible and we're blown away that you would take the time to actually vote for us,' gushed the boys. 'Three MTV EMAs for Artist on the Rise, Best New and Best Push Act is extremely crazy . . . you're all unreal and amazing and awesome.' Next up, 5SOS are set to be reunited with One Direction at the 2014 American Music Awards in LA's glamorous Nokia Theatre. Nominated for Kohl's New Artist of the Year, 5SOS will even play a short set at the star-studded ceremony on 23 November. Needless to say, they are 'stoked' at the prospect. To make up for the London show they missed, 5SOS announced two upcoming appearances in the UK: Capital's Jingle Bell Ball (London, 7 December) and radiocity96.7's Christmas Live (Liverpool, 10 December). These, of course, will be slotted into their already hectic schedule of gigs over in the States. The most thrilling of these will be z100's Jingle Ball – a glitzy, festive extravaganza that takes over New York's Madison Square Garden every Christmas. Sharing the stage with such pop royalty as Taylor Swift, Ariana Grande, Maroon 5 and Jessie J, the 12 December gig promises to be a landmark event in 5SOS's incredible career to date – providing a taste of the glittering future that's now well within reach for the four Sydney boys . . .

Aside from Ash's appendicitis, 2014 has been a truly wondrous year in 5SOS history. They've headlined tours in the UK, Australia and America; scored a UK number one with 'She Looks So Perfect' and witnessed their debut album sell in phenomenal quantities around the world. 2015 promises to be better still. Though opening night is still months away, many dates on the Rock Out with Your Socks Out tour are already sold out. But perhaps most importantly of all, Luke, Michael, Calum and Ash have shown the world they possess the showmanship, the songs and the talent to back up the hype.

British Library Cataloguing in Publication Data
A catalogue record for this book is available from
the British Library

ISBN-13: 978-0-85965-532-3

Book and cover design by Coco Balderrama
Printed in Great Britain by Bell & Bain Ltd, Glasgow

Acknowledgements
Professional thanks to Sandra Wake, Laura Coulman, April
James, Coco Balderrama and Joe Dowley at Plexus for their
assistance in helping to bring the book in on schedule.

Personal thanks to Tasha 'Bodacious Babe' Cowen
and Shannon 'Mini-B' Stanley for once again keeping the
tea flowing and the sweetie bowl brimming, Lisa 'T-Bag'
Bird, Paul Young (not the singer), Elle '5SOS' Cowen,
Beccy Boo, Alex Jones, Amun James, James Willment,
and Joel and Aggie.

The members of 5 Seconds of Summer have given
innumerable interviews to newspapers, magazines,
websites, television and radio. The author and editors
would like to thank: The Ellen DeGeneres Show, Today,
The X Factor Australia, This Morning, Australian Idol,
Radio 1, Capital FM, Radio City 96.7, MTV UK, MTV,
z100 New York, Live Nation, Nickelodeon, Hallam FM,
HMV, Modest Management, Radio Nova, KIIS 106.5,
the Daily Mail, the Guardian, the Sun, the Sydney Morning
Herald, Billboard magazine, BBC News, the Independent,
Rock Sound, Kerrang!, Rolling Stone, J-14 magazine, People,
Music Network, POPSTAR!, 60 Minutes, Cioè, the Herald
Sun, Alternative Press, Alter the Press!, the Australian Daily
Telegraph, the Huffington Post, Fuse, Seventeen, Coup de
Main, Top of the Pops, Vevo magazine, USA Today, Extra,
Hollywood Life, Hot Hits, Digital Spy, Jimmy Kimmel Live, the
New York Daily News, Pop Crush, 5sos.com, ellentv.com,
today.com, capitalfm.com, bbc.co.uk/radio1, radiocity.
co.uk, smh.com.au, Sugarscape.com, wattpad.com, twitter.
com, Facebook.com, 5sos-at-heart.tumblr.com, 5sos.wikia.
com, youtube.com, 5sos-official.tumblr.com, billboard.
com, pinterest.com, Instagram.com/5sos, lyricsmania.com,
roadtoderpcon.com, 5sosderpcon.com, dailymail.co.uk,
uk.mtvema.com, bbc.co.uk, thegarden.com, livenation.
com, hollywoodlife.com, ryanseacrest.com, setlist.fm,
azlyrics.com, foursquare.com, independent.co.uk, popsugar.
com, teenchoiceawards.com, snapchat.com, rocksound.tv,
onepopz.com, hellyesashtonirwin.tumblr.com, thefactsite.
com, inpublishing.co.uk, hmv.com, Rollingstone.com,
J-14.com, popstaronline.com, unreality.tv, popcrush.com,
modestmanagement.com, heyirwin14.tumblr.com, rebloggy.
com, New.com.au, chewdio.tumblr.com, pressparty.com,
heraldsun.com.au, astrology.com, Gulfnews.com, liveguide.
com.au, norwest.nsw.edu.au, 5sosfan.com, koko.uk.com,
altpress.com, hitzoneonline.com, 99.7now.cbslocal.com,
dailytelegraph.com.au, huffingtonpost.com, seventeen.com,
andpop.com and thoughtcatalog.com.

We would like to thank the following agencies for
photographs: Cover photograph by Getty Images/Shirlaine
Forrest/WireImage; Getty Images/Larry Marano; Getty
Images/Larry Busacca/Billboard Awards 2014; Rex/
MediaPunch; Getty Images/Michael Tran/FilmMagic;
Rex/IBL; Rex/MediaPunch; Rex/Olycom SPA; Getty
Images/Scott Legato; Getty Images/C Brandon/Redferns;
Getty Images/Stefania D'Alessandro; Getty Images/Isaac
Brekken/Billboard Awards 2014/; Shutterstock.com/Kobby
Dagan; Rex/Steve Meddle/ITV; Getty Images/Christopher
Polk/Billboard Awards 2014; Getty Images/Stephen
Lovekin/Stringer/Getty Images for Clear Channel Media
+ Entertainment; Getty Images/Mindy Small/WireImage;
Shutterstock.com/Helga Esteb; Getty Images/Kevin Mazur/
Billboard Awards 2014/WireImage; Rex/Steve Meddle/
ITV; Rex/Beretta/Sims; Rex/Everett Collection; Getty
Images/Chance Yeh/FilmMagic; Getty Images/Shirlaine
Forrest/WireImage Getty Images/John Lamparski/Stringer;
Rex/MediaPunch; Getty Images/Geoff Jones/Fairfax
Media; Rex/Steve Meddle/ITV; Rex/James McCauley;
Getty Images/Kevin Winter/Billboard Awards 2014; Getty
Images/Kevin Mazur/OneD; Getty Images/Ethan Miller/
Staff; Rex/Steve Meddle/ITV; Getty Images/Marc Piasecki/
GC Images; Getty Images/Christopher Polk/MTV1415;
Getty Images/Robin Marchant; Rex/James McCauley;
Getty Images/Cindy Ord; Rex/Broadimage; Getty Images/
Noam Galai/WireImage; Shutterstock.com/Debby Wong;
Getty Images/Tim P. Whitby/Stringer; Rex/McPix Ltd;
Getty Images/Jo Hale/RedFerns; Getty Images/Jason
Kempin; Getty Images/David M. Benett; Rex/Broadimage;
Getty Images/Steve Granitz/WireImage; Rex/Jim Smeal/
BEI; Getty Images/Jeff Kravitz/MTV1415/FilmMagic;
Shutterstock.com/Ihnatovich Maryia; Shutterstock.com/
welcomia; Shutterstock.com/Prezoom.nl; Shutterstock.
com/Nik Merkulov; Shutterstock.com/andreasnikolas;
Shutterstock.com/amgun; Shutterstock.com/Nicemonkey.